QUICK AND EASY
NOODLES

QUICK AND EASY
NOODLES

NOODLE KNOW-HOW IN DELICIOUSLY AROMATIC DISHES

Kit Chan

H
HERMES
HOUSE

This edition first published by Hermes House
an imprint of
Anness Publishing Limited
Hermes House
88–89 Blackfriars Road
London SE1 8HA

© 1996, 2000 Anness Publishing Limited

ISBN 1-84038-674-6

A CIP catalogue record for this book is available from the British Library

Publisher: Joanna Lorenz
Senior Cookery Editor: Linda Fraser
Copy Editor: Jenni Fleetwood
Designer: Ian Sandom
Photography and Styling: Thomas Odulate
Food for photography: Kit Chan, assisted by Lucy McKelvie
Illustrator: Madeleine David

Front cover: Nicki Dowey, Photographer and Stylist;
Emma Patmore, Home Economist

Previously published as part of the *Creative Cooking Library*

Printed in Hong Kong/China

1 3 5 7 9 10 8 6 4 2

NOTES

For all recipes, quantities are given in both metric and imperial measures and,
where appropriate, measures are also given in standard cups and spoons. Follow
one set, but not a mixture because they are not interchangeable.

Standard spoon and cup measurements are level.
1 tsp = 5ml, 1 tbsp = 15ml, 1 cup = 250ml/8fl oz

Medium eggs should be used unless otherwise stated.

Australian standard tablespoons are 20ml. Australian readers should use 3 tsp in
place of 1 tbsp for measuring small quantities of gelatine, cornflour, salt etc.

CONTENTS

Introduction 6

Starters *11*

Noodle Salads *23*

Satisfying Soups *35*

Snacks and Suppers *43*

Vegetarian Noodle Dishes *53*

Fast Fried Noodles *65*

Special Occasion Noodles *77*

Sweet Surprises *89*

Index *96*

INTRODUCTION

Noodles have universal appeal. Although thousands of words have been written on the subject, it is the Italian influence that prevails in most pasta cookbooks; scant mention is made of the ever-growing popularity of noodle dishes from China, Japan, Thailand and other Asian Countries.

There has been much speculation about whether the Chinese invented noodles before the Italians discovered spaghetti. One theory is that when Marco Polo journeyed overland to China late in the thirteenth century, he brought the secret of pasta-making back to his native Italy. This seems a plausible scenario; noodles were certainly known in China before the start of the Christian era. Soon after the Chinese learned how to grind grains into flour, they discovered that by adding liquid they could make dough which could be kneaded and rolled into thin sheets. It was a short step to cutting the sheets into ribbons and cooking them in boiling water. Noodles rapidly became a staple food, not only in China but throughout the entire Far East.

Noodles play an important role in many traditional festivities. In China they are a symbol of longevity and are often eaten at birthday celebrations and as "crossing of the threshold of the year" food. They are eaten at happy and sad occasions, at weddings and funerals, between meals, standing up or sitting down. You could say noodles are the oldest form of fast food in the East. Step outside a railway station in an Asian city and you are never far away from a noodle booth.

Asian pasta includes a wide variety of noodles, ranging from fine and thin to coarse and thick. Many are made with wheat flour, with or without egg. Most of these varieties are softer and starchier than their Italian counterparts, and are sold fresh or dried. Other varieties, cellophane or glass noodles, for instance, are based on vegetable starch, such as that derived from mung beans. Rice flour is used for rice sticks or vermicelli and also paper-thin rice sheets. Of the many varieties of Asian pasta, the most familiar ones are the Chinese wontons and Japanese udon, soba and somen noodles. The range of noodle types is extensive, although the Asians have never felt the need to produce as many varied shapes of pasta as the Italians have devised.

Another characteristic of Asian noodle dishes is their diversity. They can be – and are – cooked, mixed, blended and combined with just about every variety of meat, seafood and vegetables. Eaten hot or cold, they are used in soups, salads and stir-fries. They can also be braised, deep fried or made into noodle nests and cakes. In short, noodles can be served in innumerable ways, as side dishes, snacks, garnishes or complete meals. Whatever the time of day, they are perfect for everyday eating and informal entertaining, and can be enjoyed by people of all nationalities.

Noodles, deep fried until crisp, then combined with bean-sprouts, prawns, strips of chicken and a salty, chilli-flavoured sauce, are piled high to make a spectacular presentation.

EQUIPMENT

No elaborate equipment is required to prepare the dishes in this book. A cleaver, chopping block, spatula and chopsticks are basic utensils that all Asian kitchens have. You would find a draining spoon useful and will certainly need a wok.

WOK

This all-purpose cooking pan, round in shape with high sides, distributes the heat evenly and allows ingredients to be stirred and tossed without spilling. Woks come in a range of sizes and are made from various metals. Traditional woks are made of thin metal and work best on gas cookers, but you can also purchase flat bottomed woks for electric cookers. The wok's versatility is limitless. It is ideal for both stir-frying and deep frying because of its shape. It requires less oil than a flat bottomed deep fryer and has more depth and cooking surface. It can also be used for shallow frying, poaching, boiling and, with the lid, for steaming and braising.

DRAINING SPOONS

For deep frying you will need either a large twisted wire draining spoon with a wooden handle, or a metal spider to lift food out of the hot oil.

CLEAVER KNIFE

This all-purpose Chinese cutting tool looks like a butcher's cleaver. There are several kinds: stainless steel looks good, however, carbon steel holds a better edge and is easier to sharpen, but will rust; wooden handled cleavers are also available in different sizes. Lightweight cleavers are used only for slicing. Heavier cleavers, are more versatile and can also be used to chop bones. The handle is useful for pounding or mashing.

CHOPSTICKS

These can be used to replace spoons, forks and whisks. Wooden chopsticks are best for cooking because they can withstand high temperatures.

Noodle equipment, clockwise from top left: large twisted wire draining spoon, wok and chopsticks, heavy cleaver knife and metal spider

SAFETY FIRST

Oil catches fire easily when overheated and can inflict serious burns. Never fill a pan more than one-third full, keep the handle out of the way and never leave a pan of hot oil unsupervised. Oil for deep frying should cover the food by at least 2cm/³⁄₄in and should be heated to 190°C/375°F (or until a cube of dry bread, added to the oil, browns in 30 seconds). Food should always be fried in small batches to avoid overcrowding the pan, which causes the temperature to drop. Always lower food carefully into the fat, using a wire basket or slotted spoon. The food should be as dry as possible, as hot oil will spatter on contact with water. Never pour water on an oil fire.

In the event of a fire, do not panic. Turn off the heat if it is safe to do so, and cover the pan tightly to exclude air; a fire blanket is ideal for this, but a large pan lid or a baking sheet would do. If you have not already turned off the heat, do so as soon as the flames have been smothered sufficiently. Do not move the pan.

TYPES OF NOODLES

CELLOPHANE NOODLES
Made from ground mung beans, these are commonly called bean thread, transparent or glass noodles. Dried noodles must be soaked in hot water before cooking.

EGG NOODLES
Egg noodles are made from wheat flour, egg and water. The dough is flattened and then shredded or extruded through a pasta machine to the required shape and thickness.

RICE NOODLES
Banh Trang are made from ground rice and water. They range in thickness from very thin to wide ribbons and sheets. Dried ribbon rice noodles are usually sold tied together in bundles. Fresh rice noodles are also available. Rinse rice noodles in warm water and drain before use.

RICE VERMICELLI
These thin, brittle noodles look like white hair, and are sold in large bundles. Rice vermicelli cooks almost instantly in hot liquid, provided the noodles are first soaked in warm water. They can also be deep fried.

SOBA NOODLES
Made from a mixture of buckwheat and wheat flour these noodles are very popular in Japan. They are traditionally cooked in simmering water, then drained and served hot in winter or cold in summer with a dipping sauce.

SOMEN NOODLES
These delicate, thin white Japanese noodles made from wheat flour come in dried form, usually tied in bundles held together with a paper band.

UDON NOODLES
Wheat flour and water are used to make these Japanese noodles. They are usually round, but can also be flat and are available fresh, precooked or dried.

Fresh noodles, clockwise from top left: wonton wrappers, Shanghai noodles, fresh rice noodles, medium egg noodles, thin egg noodles and, centre, ribbon noodles

FRESH INGREDIENTS

BEAN CURD
Bean curd is also known as *tofu* or *dofu* and is highly nutritious. The flavourless curd blends beautifully with other ingredients. Fresh, long-life and deep-fried varieties are available.

BEANSPROUTS
High in protein and very nutritious. These can be eaten raw or cooked.

BOK CHOY
This Chinese cabbage has thick white stalks and dark green leaves.

CHINESE CHIVES
Better known as garlic chives, these are sometimes sold with their flowers.

CORIANDER
Also known as *Chinese parsley* or *cilantro*, this leafy green herb is a common accompaniment to meat and fish.

GINGER
An aromatic rhizome widely available in supermarkets. It gives a subtle piquancy to fish, meat and vegetables.

LEMON GRASS
An aromatic tropical grass that characterizes Thai and Vietnamese cuisine, lemon grass gets its name from its very distinctive scent and flavour. Crush lemon grass lightly before slicing or chopping to release more flavour.

WHEAT NOODLES

Sometimes called Shanghai noodles, these are made from wheat, water and salt. They are made in the same way as ordinary egg noodles but are whiter in colour.

WONTON WRAPPERS

Small square sheets rolled from egg noodle dough, these are available in packets from Chinese food markets.

NOODLE KNOW-HOW

All dried noodles should be stored in airtight containers where they can be kept for many months.

Fresh noodles can be chilled for several days in the plastic bag in which they were purchased (check use-by dates on packaging).

As a general rule, allow 75–115g/ 3–4oz noodles per person.

Many recipes call for noodles to be cooked twice – first par-boiled and then stir-fried or simmered in a soup or sauce. Where this is the case, the preliminary cooking should be brief. Remove the noodles from the heat when they are barely tender, immediately drain them in a colander and rinse under cold running water to arrest the cooking process. Separate the noodles with a fork and add a dash of oil if not using at once. Par-boiled noodles can be prepared in advance. They will keep for several days if stored in a tightly sealed container in the fridge.

Dried noodles, clockwise from top left: ribbon noodles, somen noodles, udon noodles, soba noodles, egg ribbon noodles, medium egg noodles, cellophane noodles, rice sheets, rice vermicelli, egg noodles, and, centre, rice ribbon noodles

STORECUPBOARD INGREDIENTS

HOISIN SAUCE

Also known as barbecue sauce, hoisin sauce is thick, dark brown, savoury/ sweet and tangy.

DRIED MUSHROOMS

Dried Chinese black mushrooms, cloud ears and wood ears become meaty and succulent when soaked in water.

OYSTER SAUCE

This thickish, slightly sweet and salty brown sauce is made from oyster extract, soy sauce, sugar and vinegar. It is used to flavour all sorts of meat, fish and vegetable dishes.

RICE WINE

Made from fermented glutinous rice, this golden wine is used for both drinking and cooking.

SESAME OIL

Extracted from toasted sesame seeds, this aromatic oil has a nutty flavour.

SOY SAUCE

An essential ingredient in Chinese cooking, soy sauce enhances the flavour of meat, fish and vegetable dishes and sauces. It ranges in colour from pale to dark, the light soy sauce having more flavour than the sweeter dark variety.

STARTERS

The versatility of noodles is amply
illustrated in this selection of tasty
starters and snacks. Whether you opt
for crunchy lettuce leaves filled with
teriyaki duck and sesame noodles, pack
up a picnic with rice noodle and salad
rolls from Vietnam, or settle for hot
chilli squid and cellophane noodles,
you'll find plenty to please. Inspiration
comes from Thailand, Japan, China
and Vietnam – and there's even a
recipe for tasty cheese fritters which
wraps an Italian treat in wonton for a
deliciously different snack.

Lettuce Wraps with Sesame Noodles

INGREDIENTS

Serves 4

15ml/1 tbsp vegetable oil
2 duck breasts, about 225g/8oz
  each, trimmed
60ml/4 tbsp saké
60ml/4 tbsp soy sauce
30ml/2 tbsp mirin
15ml/1 tbsp sugar
½ cucumber, halved, seeded and
  finely diced
30ml/2 tbsp chopped red onion
2 red chillies, seeded and
  finely chopped
30ml/2 tbsp rice vinegar
115g/4oz rice vermicelli, soaked in
  warm water until soft
15ml/1 tbsp dark sesame oil
15ml/1 tbsp black sesame
  seeds, toasted
handful of coriander leaves
12–16 large green or red
  lettuce leaves
handful of mint leaves
salt and freshly ground black pepper

1 Heat the oil in a large frying pan, add the duck breasts, skin side down and fry until golden. Turn each breast and fry the other side briefly. Remove the duck, rinse under hot water to remove excess oil, then drain.

2 Combine the saké, soy sauce, mirin and sugar in saucepan large enough to hold both duck breasts in a single layer. Bring to the boil, add the duck, skin side down, lower the heat and simmer for 3–5 minutes, depending on the thickness of the duck. Remove the pan from the heat and allow the duck to cool in the liquid.

3 Using a slotted spoon, transfer the duck to a board then slice thinly using a large sharp knife. Return the pan to a low heat and cook the sauce until it reduces and thickens slightly.

4 In a serving bowl, mix the diced cucumber with the red onion, chillies and rice vinegar. Set aside.

5 Cook the noodles in a saucepan of boiling water for about 3 minutes or until tender. Drain and rinse under cold running water. Drain again, then tip into a serving bowl and toss lightly with the sesame oil and seeds. Season with salt and pepper.

6 Place the thickened sauce and coriander leaves in separate serving bowls, alongside the bowls of noodles and the cucumber mixture. Arrange the lettuce leaves and sliced duck on individual serving plates.

7 To serve, place a few slices of duck, some noodles, cucumber, herbs and sauce inside a lettuce leaf, wrap and eat.

Rice Vermicelli and Salad Rolls

Goi Cuor is a hearty noodle salad wrapped in rice sheets: it makes a healthy change from a sandwich and is great for a picnic.

INGREDIENTS

Makes 8

50g/2oz rice vermicelli, soaked in
   warm water until soft
1 large carrot, shredded
15ml/1 tbsp sugar
15–30ml/1–2 tbsp fish sauce
8 x 20cm/8in round rice sheets
8 large lettuce leaves, thick
   stalks removed
350g/12oz Chinese roast pork, sliced
115g/4oz beansprouts
handful of mint leaves
8 cooked king prawns, peeled,
   deveined and halved
½ cucumber, cut into fine strips
coriander leaves, to garnish

For the peanut sauce
15ml/1 tbsp vegetable oil
3 garlic cloves, finely chopped
1–2 red chillies, finely chopped
5ml/1 tsp tomato purée
120ml/4fl oz/½ cup water
15ml/1 tbsp smooth peanut butter
30ml/2 tbsp hoisin sauce
2.5ml/½ tsp sugar
juice of 1 lime
50g/2oz roasted peanuts, ground

1 Drain the noodles. Cook in a saucepan of boiling water for about 2–3 minutes until tender. Drain, rinse under cold running water, drain well. Tip into a bowl. Add the carrot and season with the sugar and fish sauce.

2 Assemble the rolls, one at a time. Dip a rice sheet in a bowl of warm water, then lay it flat on a surface. Place 1 lettuce leaf, 1–2 scoops of the noodle mixture, a few slices of pork, some of the beansprouts and several mint leaves on the rice sheet.

3 Start rolling up the rice sheet into a cylinder. When half the sheet has been rolled up, fold both sides of the sheet towards the centre and lay 2 pieces of prawn along the crease.

4 Add a few of strips of cucumber and some of the coriander leaves. Continue to roll up the sheet to make a tight packet. Place the roll on a plate and cover with a damp dish towel, so that it will stay moist while you make the remaining rolls.

5 Make the peanut sauce. Heat the oil in a small saucepan and fry the garlic, chillies and tomato purée for about 1 minute. Add the water and bring to the boil, then stir in the peanut butter, hoisin sauce, sugar and lime juice. Mix well. Reduce the heat and simmer for 3–4 minutes. Spoon the sauce into a bowl, add the ground peanuts and cool to room temperature.

6 To serve, cut each roll in half. Add a spoonful of the peanut sauce.

Lettuce with Peanut Dressing and Wonton Crisps

INGREDIENTS

Serves 4

8 wonton wrappers
oil for frying
2 Little Gem lettuces, separated
    into leaves
½ cucumber, halved, seeded and cut
    into 1cm/½in dice
2 ripe tomatoes, peeled, seeded and cut
    into 1cm/½in dice
1 hard-boiled egg,
    roughly chopped
50g/2oz roasted peanuts,
    roughly chopped

For the peanut dressing

15ml/1 tbsp smooth
    peanut butter
120ml/4fl oz/½ cup coconut milk
5ml/1 tsp sugar
juice of 1 lime
few drops of Tabasco sauce
salt and freshly ground black pepper

1 Make the peanut dressing by combining the peanut butter, coconut milk and sugar together in a small saucepan. Stir over a low heat just until blended.

2 Remove the pan from the heat, stir in the lime juice and Tabasco sauce, then season with salt and pepper to taste. Set aside and leave to cool to room temperature.

3 Separate the wonton wrappers; restack them and cut into four.

4 Heat the oil in a deep saucepan or wok. When hot, add the wontons a few at a time and fry until browned. Lift them out of the oil using a slotted spoon and drain on kitchen paper. (The wontons will colour very quickly; take care not to burn them.)

5 Arrange the lettuce leaves on serving plates or bowls. Drizzle with the peanut dressing and scatter the cucumber, tomatoes, egg and peanuts on top. Lastly, add the wonton crisps and serve at once.

Somen Noodles with Baked Cherry Tomatoes

This summery dish is bursting with flavour. Baking the cherry tomatoes slowly strengthens their taste. If you can find yellow tomatoes, use half and half – the dish will look extra special.

INGREDIENTS

Serves 4–6

1kg/2¼lb cherry tomatoes
3 garlic cloves, finely sliced
1 bunch basil
120ml/4fl oz/½ cup extra virgin
    olive oil
450g/1lb somen noodles
salt and freshly ground black pepper
shavings of Parmesan cheese and tiny
    basil sprigs, to garnish (optional)

1 Preheat the oven to 180°C/350°F/ Gas 4. Cut the tomatoes in half and arrange, cut side up, in a single layer in a baking dish. Season with salt and pepper and sprinkle with sliced garlic. Strip the basil leaves from the stems, then arrange half over the tomatoes; drizzle the olive oil over the top. Bake the tomatoes for 1–1½ hours. Set aside in a cool place until ready to serve.

2 Just before serving, cook the somen noodles in a saucepan of boiling salted water until just tender, following the directions on the packet. Drain well, tip into a bowl and toss lightly with the baked tomatoes and their juices. Add the remaining basil, with more olive oil and seasoning. Serve at once, garnished with Parmesan shavings and a few basil sprigs, if liked.

Seared Scallops with Wonton Crisps

Quick seared scallops with crisp vegetables in a lightly spiced sauce make a delightful starter.

INGREDIENTS

Serves 4
16 medium scallops, halved
oil for deep frying
8 wonton wrappers
45ml/3 tbsp olive oil
1 large carrot, cut into long thin strips
1 large leek, cut into long thin strips
juice of 1 lemon
juice of ½ orange
2 spring onions, finely sliced
30ml/2 tbsp coriander leaves
salt and freshly ground black pepper

For the marinade
5ml/1 tsp Thai red curry paste
5ml/1 tsp grated fresh root ginger
1 garlic clove, finely chopped
15ml/1 tbsp soy sauce
15ml/1 tbsp olive oil

1 Make the marinade by mixing all the ingredients in a bowl. Add the scallops, toss to coat and leave to marinate for about 30 minutes.

2 Heat the oil in a large heavy-based saucepan or deep fryer and deep fry the wonton wrappers in small batches until crisp and golden.

3 When the wrappers are ready, drain them on kitchen paper and set aside until required.

4 Heat half the olive oil in a large frying pan. Add the scallops, with the marinade, and sear over a high heat for about 1 minute or until golden, taking care not to overcook (they should feel firm to the touch but not rubbery). Using a slotted spoon, transfer the scallops to a plate.

5 Add the remaining olive oil to the pan. When hot, add the carrot and leek strips. Toss and turn the vegetables until they start to wilt and soften, but remain crisp. Season to taste with salt and pepper, stir in the lemon and orange juices, and add a little more soy sauce if needed.

6 Return the scallops to the pan, mix lightly with the vegetables and heat for just long enough to warm through. Transfer to a bowl and add the spring onions and coriander. To serve, sandwich a quarter of the mixture between two wonton crisps. Make three more "sandwiches" in the same way and serve at once.

Vietnamese Spring Rolls with Nuoc Cham Sauce

INGREDIENTS

Makes 25
6 dried Chinese mushrooms, soaked
  in hot water for 30 minutes
225g/8oz lean ground pork
115g/4oz uncooked prawns, peeled,
  deveined and chopped
115g/4oz white crabmeat,
  picked over
1 carrot, shredded
50g/2oz cellophane noodles, soaked
  in water, drained and cut into
  short lengths
4 spring onions, finely sliced
2 garlic cloves, finely chopped
30ml/2 tbsp fish sauce
juice of 1 lime
freshly ground black pepper
25 x 10cm/4in Vietnamese
  rice sheets
oil for deep frying
lettuce leaves, cucumber slices and
  coriander leaves, to garnish

For the nuoc cham sauce
2 garlic cloves, finely chopped
30ml/2 tbsp white wine vinegar
juice of 1 lime
30ml/2 tbsp sugar
120ml/4fl oz/½ cup fish sauce
120ml/4fl oz/½ cup water
2 red chillies, seeded and chopped

1 Drain the mushrooms, squeezing out the excess moisture. Remove the stems and thinly slice the caps into a bowl. Add the pork, prawns, crabmeat, carrot, cellophane noodles, spring onions and garlic.

2 Season with the fish sauce, lime juice and pepper. Set the mixture aside for about 30 minutes to allow the flavours to blend.

3 Meanwhile make the nuoc cham sauce. Mix together the garlic, vinegar, lime juice, sugar, fish sauce, water and chillies in a serving bowl, then cover and set aside.

4 Assemble the spring rolls. Place a rice sheet on a flat surface and brush with warm water until it is pliable. Place about 10ml/2 tsp of the filling near the edge of the rice sheet. Fold the sides over the filling, fold in the two ends, then roll up, sealing the ends of the roll with a little water. Make more rolls in the same way until all the filling is used up.

5 Heat the oil for deep frying to 180°C/350°F or until a cube of dry bread added to the oil browns in 30–45 seconds. Add the rolls, a few at a time, and fry until golden brown and crisp. Drain on kitchen paper. Serve the spring rolls hot, garnished with the lettuce, cucumber and coriander. Offer the nuoc cham sauce separately.

Cheese Fritters

These crisp fritters owe their inspiration to Italy. A note of caution – do be careful not to burn your mouth when you take your first bite, as the soft, rich cheese filling will be very hot.

INGREDIENTS

Makes 15–16

115g/4oz ricotta cheese
50g/2oz fontina cheese, grated
25g/1oz Parmesan cheese, finely grated
pinch of cayenne pepper
1 egg, beaten, plus a little extra to seal the wontons
15–16 wonton wrappers
oil for deep frying

1 Line a large baking sheet with greaseproof paper or sprinkle it lightly with flour. Set aside. Combine the cheeses in a bowl, then add the cayenne and beaten egg and mix well.

2 Place one wonton wrapper at a time on a board. Brush the edges with egg. Spoon a little filling in the centre; pull the top corner down to the bottom corner, to make a triangle.

3 Transfer the filled wontons to the prepared baking sheet.

4 Heat the oil in a deep-fryer or large saucepan. Slip in as many wontons at one time as can be accommodated without overcrowding. Fry them for 2–3 minutes on each side or until the fritters are golden. Remove with a slotted spoon. Drain on kitchen paper and serve at once.

Chilled Soba Noodles with Nori

INGREDIENTS

Serves 4

350g/12oz dried soba noodles
1 sheet nori seaweed

For the dipping sauce

300ml/½ pint/1¼ cups bonito stock
120ml/4fl oz/½ cup dark soy sauce
60ml/4 tbsp mirin
5ml/1 tsp sugar
10g/¼ oz loose bonito flakes

Flavourings

4 spring onions, finely chopped
30ml/2 tbsp grated daikon
wasabi paste
4 egg yolks (optional)

COOK'S TIP

Daikon is a slim white vegetable, sometimes also known as mooli.

1 Make the dipping sauce. Combine the stock, soy sauce, mirin and sugar in a saucepan. Bring rapidly to the boil, add the bonito flakes, then remove from the heat. When cool, strain the sauce into a bowl and cover. (This can be done in advance and the sauce kept chilled for up to a week.)

2 Cook the soba noodles in a saucepan of lightly salted boiling water for 6–7 minutes or until just tender, following the manufacturer's directions on the packet.

3 Drain and rinse the noodles under cold running water, agitating them gently to remove the excess starch. Drain well.

4 Toast the nori over a high gas flame or under a hot grill, then crumble into thin strips. Divide the noodles among four serving dishes and top with the nori. Serve each portion with an individual bowl of dipping sauce and offer the flavourings separately.

Seafood Wontons with Coriander Dressing

These tasty wontons resemble tortellini. Water chestnuts add a light crunch to the filling.

INGREDIENTS

Serves 4
225g/8oz raw prawns, peeled
  and deveined
115g/4oz white crabmeat, picked over
4 canned water chestnuts, finely diced
1 spring onion, finely chopped
1 small green chilli, seeded and
  finely chopped
1.25ml/½ tsp grated fresh root ginger
20–24 wonton wrappers
1 egg, separated
salt and freshly ground black pepper
coriander leaves, to garnish

For the coriander dressing
30ml/2 tbsp rice vinegar
15ml/1 tbsp chopped pickled ginger
90ml/6 tbsp olive oil
15ml/1 tbsp soy sauce
45ml/3 tbsp chopped coriander
30ml/2 tbsp finely diced red pepper

1 Finely dice the prawns and place them in a bowl. Add the crabmeat, water chestnuts, spring onion, chilli, ginger and egg white. Season with salt and pepper and stir well.

2 Place a wonton wrapper on a board. Put about 5ml/1 tsp of the filling just above the centre of the wrapper. With a pastry brush, moisten the edges of the wrapper with a little of the egg yolk. Bring the bottom of the wrapper up over the filling. Press gently to expel any air, then seal the wrapper neatly in a triangle.

3 For a more elaborate shape, bring the two side points up over the filling, overlap the points and pinch the ends firmly together. Space the filled wontons on a large baking sheet lined with greaseproof paper, so that they do not stick together.

4 Half fill a large saucepan with water. Bring to simmering point. Add the filled wontons, a few at a time, and simmer for 2–3 minutes. The wontons will float to the surface. When ready the wrappers will be translucent and the filling should be cooked. Remove the wontons with a large slotted spoon, drain them briefly, then spread them on trays. Keep warm while cooking the remaining wontons.

5 Make the coriander dressing by whisking all the ingredients together in a bowl. Divide the wontons among serving dishes, drizzle with the dressing and serve garnished with a handful of coriander leaves.

Clay Pot of Chilli Squid and Noodles

INGREDIENTS

Serves 4

675g/1½lb fresh squid
30ml/2 tbsp vegetable oil
3 slices fresh root ginger,
  finely shredded
2 garlic cloves, finely chopped
1 red onion, finely sliced
1 carrot, finely sliced
1 celery stick, diagonally sliced
50g/2oz sugar snap peas, topped
  and tailed
5ml/1 tsp sugar
15ml/1 tbsp chilli bean paste
2.5ml/½ tsp chilli powder
75g/3oz cellophane noodles, soaked in
  hot water until soft
120ml/4fl oz/½ cup chicken stock
  or water
15ml/1 tbsp soy sauce
15ml/1 tbsp oyster sauce
5ml/1 tsp sesame oil
pinch of salt
coriander leaves, to garnish

1 Prepare the squid. Holding the body in one hand, gently pull away the head and tentacles. Discard the head; trim and reserve the tentacles. Remove the transparent "quill" from inside the body of the squid. Peel off the brown skin on the outside of the body. Rub a little salt into the squid and wash thoroughly under cold running water. Cut the body of the squid into rings or split it open lengthways, score criss-cross patterns on the inside of the body and cut it into 5 x 4cm/2 x 1½ in pieces.

2 Heat the oil in a large clay pot or flameproof casserole. Add the ginger, garlic and onion, and fry for 1–2 minutes. Add the squid, carrot, celery and sugar snap peas. Fry until the squid curls up. Season with salt and sugar, and stir in the chilli bean paste and powder. Transfer the mixture to a bowl and set aside until required.

3 Drain the soaked noodles and add them to the clay pot or casserole. Stir in the stock or water, soy sauce and oyster sauce. Cover and cook over a medium heat for about 10 minutes or until the noodles are tender.

4 Return the squid and vegetables to the pot. Cover and cook for about 5–6 minutes more, until all the flavours are combined. Season to taste.

5 Just before serving, drizzle with the sesame oil and sprinkle with the coriander leaves.

--- COOK'S TIP ---

These noodles have a smooth, light texture that readily absorbs the other flavours in the dish. To vary the flavour, the vegetables can be altered according to what is available.

NOODLE SALADS

Noodle salads are delicious and easy to make. Serve one as a starter, a side dish or – with the addition of meat, fish or vegetables – as a satisfying light lunch. The texture of the noodles is important. Remove them from the heat as soon as they are tender, and rinse them under cold running water to stop the cooking process and remove excess starch. Most salads are best served as soon as they are made; if you must chill the salad, bring it to room temperature and adjust the seasoning before serving.

Prawn Noodle Salad with Fragrant Herbs

A light, refreshing salad with all the tangy flavour of the sea. Instead of prawns, try squid, scallops, mussels or crab.

INGREDIENTS

Serves 4

115g/4oz cellophane noodles, soaked in hot water until soft
16 cooked prawns, peeled
1 small green pepper, seeded and cut into strips
½ cucumber, cut into strips
1 tomato, cut into strips
2 shallots, finely sliced
salt and freshly ground black pepper
coriander leaves, to garnish

For the dressing

15ml/1 tbsp rice vinegar
30ml/2 tbsp fish sauce
30ml/2 tbsp fresh lime juice
pinch of salt
2.5ml/½ tsp grated fresh root ginger
1 lemon grass stalk, finely chopped
1 red chilli, seeded and finely sliced
30ml/2 tbsp roughly chopped mint
few sprigs tarragon, roughly chopped
15ml/1 tbsp snipped chives

1 Make the dressing by combining all the ingredients in a small bowl or jug; whisk well.

2 Drain the noodles, then plunge them in a saucepan of boiling water for 1 minute. Drain, rinse under cold running water and drain again well.

3 In a large bowl, combine the noodles with the prawns, pepper, cucumber, tomato and shallots. Lightly season with salt and pepper, then toss with the dressing.

4 Spoon the noodles on to individual plates, arranging the prawns on top. Garnish with a few coriander leaves and serve at once.

--- COOK'S TIP ---

Prawns are available ready-cooked and often shelled. To cook prawns, boil them for 5 minutes. Leave them to cool in the cooking liquid, then gently pull off the tail shell and twist off the head.

Smoked Trout and Noodle Salad

It is important to use ripe juicy tomatoes for this fresh–tasting salad. For a special occasion you could replace the smoked trout with smoked salmon.

INGREDIENTS

Serves 4
225g/8oz somen noodles
2 smoked trout, skinned and boned
2 hard-boiled eggs, coarsely chopped
30ml/2 tbsp snipped chives
lime halves, to serve (optional)

For the dressing
6 ripe plum tomatoes
2 shallots, finely chopped
30ml/2 tbsp tiny capers, rinsed
30ml/2 tbsp chopped fresh tarragon
finely grated rind and juice of ½ orange
60ml/4 tbsp extra virgin olive oil
salt and freshly ground black pepper

1 To make the dressing, cut the tomatoes in half, remove the cores, and cut the flesh into chunks.

2 Place in a bowl with the shallots, capers, tarragon, orange rind, orange juice and olive oil. Season with salt and pepper, and mix well. Leave the dressing to marinate at room temperature for 1–2 hours.

3 Cook the noodles in a large saucepan of boiling water until just tender. Drain and rinse under cold running water. Drain well.

5 Flake the smoked trout over the noodles, then sprinkle the coarsely chopped eggs and snipped chives over the top. Serve the lime halves on the side, if you like.

4 Toss the noodles with the dressing, then adjust the seasoning to taste. Arrange the noodles on a large serving platter or individual plates.

--- COOK'S TIP ---

Choose tomatoes that are firm, bright in colour and have a matt texture, avoiding any with blotched or cracked skins.

Spicy Szechuan Noodles

INGREDIENTS

Serves 4
350g/12oz thick noodles
175g/6oz cooked chicken,
   shredded
50g/2oz roasted cashew nuts

For the dressing
4 spring onions, chopped
30ml/2 tbsp chopped coriander
2 garlic cloves, chopped
30ml/2 tbsp smooth peanut butter
30ml/2 tbsp sweet chilli sauce
15ml/1 tbsp soy sauce
15ml/1 tbsp sherry vinegar
15ml/1 tbsp sesame oil
30ml/2 tbsp olive oil
30ml/2 tbsp chicken stock
   or water
10 toasted Szechuan peppercorns,
   ground

1 Cook the noodles in a saucepan of boiling water until just tender, following the directions on the packet. Drain, rinse under cold running water and drain well.

2 While the noodles are cooking combine all the ingredients for the dressing in a large bowl and whisk together well.

3 Add the noodles, shredded chicken and cashew nuts to the dressing, toss gently to coat and adjust the seasoning to taste. Serve at once.

COOK'S TIP

You could substitute cooked turkey or pork for the chicken for a change.

Sesame Noodles with Spring Onions

This simple but very tasty warm salad can be prepared and cooked in just a few minutes.

INGREDIENTS

Serves 4
2 garlic cloves, roughly chopped
30ml/2 tbsp Chinese sesame paste
15ml/1 tbsp dark sesame oil
30ml/2 tbsp soy sauce
30ml/2 tbsp rice wine
15ml/1 tbsp honey
pinch of five-spice powder
350g/12oz soba or
   buckwheat noodles
4 spring onions, finely
   sliced diagonally
50g/2oz beansprouts
7.5cm/3in piece of cucumber, cut
   into matchsticks
toasted sesame seeds
salt and freshly ground black pepper

1 Process the garlic, sesame paste, oil, soy sauce, rice wine, honey and five-spice powder with a pinch each of salt and pepper in a blender or food processor until smooth.

2 Cook the noodles in a saucepan of boiling water until just tender, following the directions on the packet. Drain the noodles immediately and tip them into a bowl.

3 Toss the hot noodles with the dressing and the spring onions. Top with the beansprouts, cucumber and sesame seeds and serve.

COOK'S TIP

If you can't find Chinese sesame paste, then use either tahini paste or smooth peanut butter instead.

Curry Fried Pork and Rice Vermicelli Salad

Pork crackles add a delicious crunch to this popular salad.

INGREDIENTS

Serves 4

225g/8oz lean pork
2 garlic cloves, finely chopped
2 slices fresh root ginger,
  finely chopped
30–45ml/2–3 tbsp rice wine
45ml/3 tbsp vegetable oil
2 lemon grass stalks, finely chopped
10ml/2 tsp curry powder
175g/6oz beansprouts
225g/8oz rice vermicelli, soaked in
  warm water until soft
½ lettuce, finely shredded
30ml/2 tbsp mint leaves
lemon juice and fish sauce, to taste
salt and freshly ground black pepper
2 spring onions, chopped, 25g/1oz
  roasted peanuts, chopped, and pork
  crackles (optional), to garnish

1 Cut the pork into thin strips. Place in a shallow dish with half the garlic and ginger. Season with salt and pepper, pour over 30ml/2 tbsp rice wine and marinate for at least 1 hour.

2 Heat the oil in a frying pan. Add the remaining garlic and ginger and fry for a few seconds until fragrant. Stir in the pork, with the marinade, and add the lemon grass and curry powder. Fry until the pork is golden and cooked through, adding more rice wine if the mixture seems too dry.

3 Place the beansprouts in a sieve. Blanch them by lowering the sieve into a saucepan of boiling water for 1 minute, then drain and refresh under cold running water. Drain again. Using the same water, cook the drained rice vermicelli for 3–5 minutes until tender, drain and rinse under cold running water. Drain well and tip into a bowl.

4 Add the beansprouts, shredded lettuce and mint leaves to the rice vermicelli. Season with the lemon juice and fish sauce. Toss lightly.

5 Divide the noodle mixture among individual serving plates, making a nest on each plate. Arrange the pork mixture on top. Garnish with spring onions, roasted peanuts and pork crackles, if using.

Potato and Cellophane Noodle Salad

INGREDIENTS

Serves 4

2 medium potatoes, peeled and cut
  into eighths
175g/6oz cellophane noodles, soaked
  in hot water until soft
60ml/4 tbsp vegetable oil
1 onion, finely sliced
5ml/1 tsp ground turmeric
60ml/4 tbsp gram flour
5ml/1 tsp grated lemon rind
60–75ml/4–5 tbsp lemon juice
45ml/3 tbsp fish sauce
4 spring onions, finely sliced
salt and freshly ground black pepper

1 Place the potatoes in a saucepan.
Add water to cover, bring to the
boil and cook for about 15 minutes
until tender but firm. Drain the
potatoes and set them aside to cool.

2 Meanwhile, cook the drained
noodles in a saucepan of boiling
water for 3 minutes. Drain and rinse
under cold running water. Drain well.

3 Heat the oil in a frying pan. Add
the onion and turmeric and fry for
about 5 minutes until golden brown.
Drain the onion, reserving the oil.

4 Heat a small frying pan. Add the
gram flour and stir constantly for
about 4 minutes until it turns light
golden brown in colour.

5 Mix the potatoes, noodles and fried
onion in a large bowl. Add the
reserved oil and the toasted gram flour
with the lemon rind and juice, fish
sauce and spring onions. Mix together
well and adjust the seasoning to taste if
necessary. Serve at once.

Noodles with Pineapple, Ginger and Chillies

INGREDIENTS

Serves 4

275g/10oz dried udon noodles
½ pineapple, peeled, cored and sliced
   into 4cm/1½ in rings
45ml/3 tbsp soft light brown sugar
60ml/4 tbsp fresh lime juice
60ml/4 tbsp coconut milk
30ml/2 tbsp fish sauce
30ml/2 tbsp grated fresh root ginger
2 garlic cloves, finely chopped
1 ripe mango or 2 peaches,
   finely diced
freshly ground black pepper
2 spring onions, finely sliced, 2 red
   chillies, seeded and finely shredded,
   plus mint leaves, to garnish

1 Cook the noodles in a large saucepan of boiling water until tender, following the directions on the packet. Drain, refresh under cold water and drain again.

2 Place the pineapple rings on a flameproof dish, sprinkle with 30ml/2 tbsp of the sugar and grill for about 5 minutes or until golden. Cool slightly and cut into small dice.

3 Mix the lime juice, coconut milk and fish sauce in a salad bowl. Add the remaining brown sugar, with the ginger and garlic, and whisk well. Add the noodles and pineapple.

4 Add the mango or peaches and toss. Scatter over the spring onions, chillies and mint leaves before serving.

Buckwheat Noodles with Smoked Salmon

Young pea sprouts are only available for a short time. You can substitute watercress, mustard cress, young leeks or your favourite green vegetable or herb in this dish.

INGREDIENTS

Serves 4

225g/8oz buckwheat or soba noodles
15ml/1 tbsp oyster sauce
juice of ½ lemon
30–45ml/2–3 tbsp light olive oil
115g/4oz smoked salmon, cut into
   fine strips
115g/4oz young pea sprouts
2 ripe tomatoes, peeled, seeded and cut
   into strips
15ml/1 tbsp snipped chives
salt and freshly ground black pepper

1 Cook the buckwheat or soba noodles in a large saucepan of boiling water, following the directions on the packet. Drain, then rinse under cold running water and drain well.

2 Tip the noodles into a large bowl. Add the oyster sauce and lemon juice and season with pepper to taste. Moisten with the olive oil.

3 Add the smoked salmon, pea sprouts, tomatoes and chives. Mix well and serve at once.

Egg Noodle Salad with Sesame Chicken

INGREDIENTS

Serves 4–6

400g/14oz fresh thin egg noodles
1 carrot, cut into long fine strips
50g/2oz mange-touts, topped, tailed,
   cut into fine strips and blanched
115g/4oz beansprouts, blanched
30ml/2 tbsp olive oil
225g/8oz skinless, boneless chicken
   breasts, finely sliced
30ml/2 tbsp sesame seeds, toasted
2 spring onions, finely sliced diagonally
   and coriander leaves, to garnish

For the dressing

45ml/3 tbsp sherry vinegar
75ml/5 tbsp soy sauce
60ml/4 tbsp sesame oil
90ml/6 tbsp light olive oil
1 garlic clove, finely chopped
5ml/1 tsp grated fresh root ginger
salt and freshly ground black pepper

1 To make the dressing. Combine all the ingredients in a small bowl with a pinch of salt and mix together well using a whisk or a fork.

2 Cook the noodles in a large saucepan of boiling water. Stir them occasionally to separate. They will only take a few minutes to cook: be careful not to overcook them. Drain, rinse under cold running water and drain well. Tip into a bowl.

3 Add the vegetables to the noodles. Pour in about half the dressing, then toss the mixture well and adjust the seasoning according to taste.

4 Heat the oil in a large frying pan. Add the chicken and stir-fry for 3 minutes, or until cooked and golden. Remove from the heat. Add the sesame seeds and drizzle in some of the remaining dressing.

5 Arrange the noodles on individual serving plates, making a nest on each plate. Spoon the chicken on top. Sprinkle with the sliced spring onions and the coriander leaves and serve any remaining dressing separately.

Thai Noodle Salad

The addition of coconut milk and sesame oil gives an unusual nutty flavour to the dressing for this colourful, noodle salad.

INGREDIENTS

Serves 4–6

350g/12oz somen noodles
1 large carrot, cut into thin strips
1 bunch asparagus, trimmed and cut into 4cm/1½in lengths
1 red pepper, seeded and cut into fine strips
115g/4oz mange-touts, topped, tailed and halved
115g/4oz baby corn cobs, halved lengthways
115g/4oz beansprouts
115g/4oz can water chestnuts, drained and finely sliced
1 lime, cut into wedges, 50g/2oz roasted peanuts, roughly chopped, and coriander leaves, to garnish

For the dressing
45ml/3 tbsp roughly torn basil
75ml/5 tbsp roughly chopped mint
250ml/8fl oz/1 cup coconut milk
30ml/2 tbsp dark sesame oil
15ml/1 tbsp grated fresh root ginger
2 garlic cloves, finely chopped
juice of 1 lime
2 spring onions, finely chopped
salt and cayenne pepper

COOK'S TIP

Shredded omelette or sliced hard-boiled eggs are also popular garnishes, and tuna noodle salad is a children's favourite.

1 Combine the basil, mint, coconut milk, sesame oil, ginger, garlic, lime juice and spring onions in a bowl and mix well. Season to taste with salt and cayenne pepper.

2 Cook the noodles in a saucepan of boiling water until just tender, following the directions on the packet. Drain, rinse under cold running water and drain again.

3 Cook all the vegetables in separate saucepans of boiling lightly salted water until tender but still crisp. Drain, plunge them immediately into cold water and drain again.

4 Toss the noodles, vegetables and dressing together to combine. Arrange on individual serving plates and garnish with the lime wedges, peanuts and coriander leaves.

SATISFYING SOUPS

*Hearty, fortifying noodle soup is the
wake-up call for many people in the Far
East, as well as being a quick midday
snack. Making a basic noodle soup is
simplicity itself; start with a good clear
chicken stock and add noodles and
slivers of meat, fish or vegetables. Serve
with a selection of accompaniments, such
as sliced spring onions, fresh coriander or
chopped chillies. Increase the quantity of
noodles, and the soups in this chapter
can make a complete meal. It is
traditional to use chopsticks for the
noodles – and slurping the soup is
perfectly proper; a sign of
real appreciation.*

Chicken and Buckwheat Noodle Soup

Buckwheat or soba noodles are widely enjoyed in Japan. The simplest way of serving them is in hot seasoned broth. Almost any topping can be added and the variations are endless.

INGREDIENTS

Serves 4

225g/8oz skinless, boneless
    chicken breasts
120ml/4fl oz/½ cup soy sauce
15ml/1 tbsp saké
1 litre/1¾ pints/4 cups chicken stock
2 pieces young leek, cut into
    2.5cm/1in pieces
175g/6oz spinach leaves
300g/11oz buckwheat or
    soba noodles
sesame seeds, toasted, to garnish

1 Slice the chicken diagonally into bite-size pieces. Combine the soy sauce and saké in a saucepan. Bring to a simmer. Add the chicken and cook gently for about 3 minutes until it is tender. Keep hot.

2 Bring the stock to the boil in a saucepan. Add the leek and simmer for 3 minutes, then add the spinach. Remove from the heat but keep warm.

3 Cook the noodles in a large saucepan of boiling water until just tender, following the manufacturer's directions on the packet.

4 Drain the noodles and divide among individual serving bowls. Ladle the hot soup into the bowls, then add a portion of chicken to each. Serve at once, sprinkled with sesame seeds.

— COOK'S TIP —

Home-made chicken stock makes the world of difference to noodle soup. Make a big batch of stock, use as much as you need and freeze the rest until required. Put about 1.5kg/3–3½lb meaty chicken bones into a large saucepan, add 3 litres/5 pints/12½ cups water and slowly bring to the boil, skimming off any foam that rises to the top. Add 2 slices fresh root ginger, 2 garlic cloves, 2 celery sticks, 4 spring onions, a handful of coriander stalks and about 10 peppercorns, crushed, then reduce the heat and simmer the stock for 2–2½ hours. Remove from the heat and leave to cool, uncovered and undisturbed. Strain the stock into a clean bowl, leaving the last dregs behind as they tend to cloud the soup. Use as required, removing any fat that congeals on top.

Hanoi Beef and Noodle Soup

Millions of North Vietnamese eat this fragrant soup for breakfast.

INGREDIENTS

Serves 4–6
1 onion
1.5kg/3–3½lb beef shank
    with bones
2.5cm/1in fresh root ginger
1 star anise
1 bay leaf
2 whole cloves
2.5ml/½ tsp fennel seeds
1 piece of cassia bark or
    cinnamon stick
3 litres/5 pints/12½ cups water
fish sauce, to taste
juice of 1 lime
150g/5oz fillet steak
450g/1lb fresh flat rice noodles
salt and freshly ground black pepper

Accompaniments
1 small red onion, sliced into rings
115g/4oz beansprouts
2 red chillies, seeded and sliced
2 spring onions, finely sliced
handful of coriander leaves
lime wedges

1 Cut the onion in half. Grill under a high heat, cut side up, until the exposed sides are caramelized, and deep brown. Set aside.

2 Cut the meat into large chunks and then place with the bones in a large saucepan or stock pot. Add the caramelized onion with the ginger, star anise, bay leaf, cloves, fennel seeds and cassia bark or cinnamon stick.

3 Add the water, bring to the boil, reduce the heat and simmer gently for 2–3 hours, skimming off the fat and scum from time to time.

4 Using a slotted spoon, remove the meat from the stock; when cool enough to handle, cut into small pieces, discarding the bones. Strain the stock and return to the pan or stock pot together with the meat. Bring back to the boil and season with the fish sauce and lime juice.

5 Slice the fillet steak very thinly and then chill until required. Place the accompaniments in separate bowls.

6 Cook the noodles in a large saucepan of boiling water until just tender. Drain and divide among individual serving bowls. Arrange the thinly sliced steak over the noodles, pour the hot stock on top and serve, offering the accompaniments separately so that each person may garnish their soup as they like.

Noodle Soup with Pork and Szechuan Pickle

INGREDIENTS

Serves 4

1 litre/1¾ pints/4 cups chicken stock
350g/12oz egg noodles
15ml/1 tbsp dried shrimps, soaked
   in water
30ml/2 tbsp vegetable oil
225g/8oz lean pork,
   finely shredded
15ml/1 tbsp yellow bean paste
15ml/1 tbsp soy sauce
115g/4oz Szechuan hot pickle, rinsed,
   drained and shredded
pinch of sugar
salt and freshly ground black pepper
2 spring onions, finely sliced,
   to garnish

1 Bring the stock to the boil in a large saucepan. Add the noodles and cook until almost tender. Drain the dried shrimps, rinse them under cold water, drain again and add to the stock. Lower the heat and simmer for a further 2 minutes. Keep hot. Heat the oil in a frying pan or wok. Add the pork and stir-fry over a high heat for about 3 minutes.

2 Add the bean paste and soy sauce to the pork; stir-fry for 1 minute more. Add the hot pickle with a pinch of sugar. Stir-fry for 1 minute more.

3 Divide the noodles and soup among individual serving bowls. Spoon the pork mixture on top, then sprinkle with the spring onions and serve at once.

Snapper, Tomato and Tamarind Noodle Soup

Tamarind gives this light, fragrant noodle soup a slightly sour taste.

INGREDIENTS

Serves 4

2 litres/3½ pints/8 cups water
1kg/2¼lb red snapper (or other red
   fish such as mullet)
1 onion, sliced
50g/2oz tamarind pods
15ml/1 tbsp fish sauce
15ml/1 tbsp sugar
30ml/2 tbsp vegetable oil
2 garlic cloves, finely chopped
2 lemon grass stalks, very
   finely chopped
4 ripe tomatoes, roughly chopped
30ml/2 tbsp yellow bean paste
225g/8oz rice vermicelli, soaked in
   warm water until soft
115g/4oz beansprouts
8–10 basil or mint sprigs
25g/1oz roasted peanuts, ground
salt and freshly ground black pepper

1 Bring the water to the boil in a saucepan. Lower the heat and add the fish and onion, with 2.5ml/½ tsp salt. Simmer gently until the fish is cooked through.

2 Remove the fish from the stock; set aside. Add the tamarind, fish sauce and sugar to the stock. Cook for 5 minutes, then strain the stock into a large jug or bowl. Carefully remove all of the bones from the fish, keeping the flesh in big pieces.

3 Heat the oil in a large frying pan. Add the garlic and lemon grass and fry for a few seconds. Stir in the tomatoes and bean paste. Cook gently for 5–7 minutes, until the tomatoes are soft. Add the stock, bring back to a simmer and adjust the seasoning.

4 Drain the vermicelli. Plunge it into a saucepan of boiling water for a few minutes, drain and divide among individual serving bowls. Add the beansprouts, fish, basil or mint, and sprinkle the ground peanuts on top. Top up each bowl with the hot soup.

Soupy Noodles – Malay-style

INGREDIENTS

Serves 4

15ml/1 tbsp vegetable oil
2 garlic cloves, very
  finely chopped
2 shallots, chopped
900ml/1½ pints/3¾ cups
  chicken stock
225g/8oz lean beef or pork,
  thinly sliced
150g/5oz fish balls
4 raw king prawns, peeled
  and deveined
350g/12oz egg noodles
115g/4oz watercress
salt and freshly ground black pepper

For the garnish
115g/4oz beansprouts
2 spring onions, sliced
15ml/1 tbsp coriander leaves
2 red chillies, seeded
  and chopped
30ml/2 tbsp deep-fried onions

1 Heat the oil in a saucepan, fry the garlic and shallots for 1 minute, then stir in the stock. Bring to the boil, then reduce the heat, add the beef or pork, fish balls and prawns and simmer for about 2 minutes.

--- COOK'S TIP ---

Fish balls can be purchased from Chinese food markets. Look out for beef and squid balls, if you fancy a variation on this.

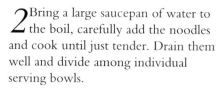

2 Bring a large saucepan of water to the boil, carefully add the noodles and cook until just tender. Drain them well and divide among individual serving bowls.

3 Season the soup with salt and pepper, then add the watercress (the hot soup will cook it instantly).

4 Scoop out the beef or pork, fish balls, prawns and watercress from the soup and arrange over the noodles. Pour the hot soup on top. Serve at once, sprinkled with a little of each of the garnishing ingredients.

Seafood Laksa

For a special occasion serve creamy rice noodles in a spicy coconut-flavoured soup, topped with seafood. There is a fair amount of work involved in the preparation but you can make the soup base ahead.

INGREDIENTS

Serves 4

4 red chillies, seeded and
  roughly chopped
1 onion, roughly chopped
1 piece *blacan*, the size of a stock cube
1 lemon grass stalk, chopped
1 small piece fresh root ginger,
  roughly chopped
6 macadamia nuts or almonds
60ml/4 tbsp vegetable oil
5ml/1 tsp paprika
5ml/1 tsp ground turmeric
475ml/16fl oz/2 cups stock or water
600ml/1 pint/2½ cups coconut milk
fish sauce (see method)
12 king prawns, peeled and deveined
8 scallops
225g/8oz prepared squid, cut
  into rings
350g/12oz rice vermicelli or rice
  noodles, soaked in warm water
  until soft
salt and freshly ground black pepper
lime halves, to serve

For the garnish
¼ cucumber, cut into matchsticks
2 red chillies, seeded and finely sliced
30ml/2 tbsp mint leaves
30ml/2 tbsp fried shallots or onions

1 In a blender or food processor, process the chillies, onion, *blacan*, lemon grass, ginger and nuts until smooth in texture.

COOK'S TIP

Blacan is dried shrimp or prawn paste. It is sold in small blocks and you will find it in oriental supermarkets.

2 Heat 45ml/3 tbsp of the oil in a large saucepan. Add the chilli paste and fry for 6 minutes. Stir in the paprika and turmeric and fry for about 2 minutes more.

3 Add the stock or water and the coconut milk to the pan. Bring to the boil, reduce the heat and simmer gently for 15–20 minutes. Season to taste with fish sauce.

4 Season the seafood with salt and pepper. Heat the remaining oil in a frying pan, add the seafood and fry quickly for 2–3 minutes until cooked.

5 Add the noodles to the soup and heat through. Divide among individual serving bowls. Place the fried seafood on top, then garnish with the cucumber, chillies, mint and fried shallots or onions. Serve with the limes.

SNACKS AND SUPPERS

Quick and easy noodles are the perfect convenience food. Keep a few packets in your pantry, along with cans of tomatoes, sardines and tuna, and you will be able to produce a healthy, nutritious meal in moments – perfect for those occasions when everyone in the family is rushing to go out, or to cater for unexpected guests. If any of the recommended ingredients are absent, improvise. Make a flavoursome sauce, add some crisp vegetables for texture, toss in your favourite noodles and enjoy a few well-deserved compliments.

Noodles with Sun-dried Tomatoes and Prawns

INGREDIENTS

Serves 4

350g/12oz somen noodles
45ml/3 tbsp olive oil
20 uncooked king prawns, peeled
   and deveined
2 garlic cloves, finely chopped
45–60ml/3–4 tbsp sun-dried
   tomato paste
salt and freshly ground black pepper

For the garnish
handful of basil leaves
30ml/2 tbsp sun-dried tomatoes in oil,
   drained and cut into strips

--- COOK'S TIP ---

Ready-made sun-dried tomato paste is readily available, however you can make your own simply by processing bottled sun-dried tomatoes with their oil. You could also add a couple of anchovy fillets and some capers if you like.

1 Cook the noodles in a large saucepan of boiling water until tender, following the directions on the packet. Drain.

2 Heat half the oil in a large frying pan. Add the prawns and garlic and fry them over a medium heat for 3–5 minutes, until the prawns turn pink and are firm to the touch.

3 Stir in 15ml/1 tbsp of the sun-dried tomato paste and mix well. Using a slotted spoon, transfer the prawns to a bowl and keep hot.

4 Reheat the oil remaining in the pan. Stir in the rest of the oil with the remaining sun-dried tomato paste. You may need to add a spoonful of water if the mixture is very thick.

5 When the mixture starts to sizzle, toss in the noodles. Add salt and pepper to taste and mix well.

6 Return the prawns to the pan and toss to combine. Serve at once garnished with the basil and strips of sun-dried tomatoes.

Chicken Chow Mein

Chow Mein is arguably the best known Chinese noodle dish in the West. Noodles are stir-fried with meat, seafood or vegetables.

INGREDIENTS

Serves 4

350g/12oz noodles
225g/8oz skinless, boneless
   chicken breasts
45ml/3 tbsp soy sauce
15ml/1 tbsp rice wine or dry sherry
15ml/1 tbsp dark sesame oil
60ml/4 tbsp vegetable oil
2 garlic cloves, finely chopped
50g/2oz mange-touts, topped
   and tailed
115g/4oz beansprouts
50g/2oz ham, finely shredded
4 spring onions, finely chopped
salt and freshly ground black pepper

1 Cook the noodles in a saucepan of boiling water until tender. Drain, rinse under cold water and drain well.

2 Slice the chicken into fine shreds about 5cm/2in in length. Place in a bowl and add 10ml/2 tsp of the soy sauce, the rice wine or sherry and sesame oil.

3 Heat half the vegetable oil in a wok or large frying pan over a high heat. When it starts smoking, add the chicken mixture. Stir-fry for 2 minutes, then transfer the chicken to a plate and keep it hot.

4 Wipe the wok clean and heat the remaining oil. Stir in the garlic, mange-touts, beansprouts and ham, stir-fry for another minute or so and add the noodles.

5 Continue to stir-fry until the noodles are heated through. Add the remaining soy sauce to taste and season with salt and pepper. Return the chicken and any juices to the noodle mixture, add the chopped spring onions and give the mixture a final stir. Serve at once.

Shanghai Noodles with Lap Cheong

Lap cheong are firm, cured waxy pork sausages, available from Chinese food markets. Sweet and savoury, they can be steamed with rice, chicken or pork, added to an omelette or stir-fried with vegetables.

INGREDIENTS

Serves 4

30ml/2 tbsp vegetable oil
115g/4oz rindless back bacon, cut into
   bite-size pieces
2 lap cheong, rinsed in warm water,
   drained and finely sliced
2 garlic cloves, finely chopped
2 spring onions, roughly chopped
225g/8oz Chinese greens or fresh
   spinach leaves, cut into
   5cm/2in pieces
450g/1lb fresh Shanghai noodles
30ml/2 tbsp oyster sauce
30ml/2 tbsp soy sauce
freshly ground black pepper

1 Heat half the oil in a wok or large frying pan. Add the bacon and lap cheong with the garlic and spring onions. Stir fry for a few minutes until golden. Using a slotted spoon, remove the mixture from the wok or pan and keep warm.

2 Add the remaining oil to the wok or pan. When hot, stir-fry the Chinese greens or spinach over a high heat for about 3 minutes until it just starts to wilt.

3 Add the noodles and return the lap cheong mixture to the wok or pan. Season with oyster sauce, soy sauce and pepper. Stir-fry until the noodles are heated through.

COOK'S TIP

You can buy rindless bacon already cut into bite-size pieces. To remove the rind from bacon rashers cut it off with sharp kitchen scissors.

Noodles with Tomatoes, Sardines and Mustard

Serve this simple dish hot or at room temperature.

INGREDIENTS

Serves 4

350g/12oz broad egg noodles
60ml/4 tbsp olive oil
30ml/2 tbsp lemon juice
15ml/1 tbsp wholegrain mustard
1 garlic clove, finely chopped
225g/8oz ripe tomatoes,
   roughly chopped
1 small red onion, finely chopped
1 green pepper, seeded and
   finely diced
60ml/4 tbsp chopped parsley
225g/8oz canned sardines, drained
salt and freshly ground black pepper
croûtons, made from 2 slices of bread,
   to serve (optional)

1 Cook the noodles in a large saucepan of boiling water for about 5–8 minutes until just tender.

2 Meanwhile, to make the dressing, whisk the oil, lemon juice, mustard and garlic in a small bowl with salt and pepper to taste.

3 Drain the noodles, tip into a large bowl and toss with the dressing. Add the tomatoes, onion, pepper, parsley and sardines and toss lightly again. Season to taste and serve with crisp croûtons, if using.

Noodles with Asparagus and Saffron Sauce

A rather elegant summery dish with fragrant saffron cream.

INGREDIENTS

Serves 4

450g/1lb young asparagus
pinch of saffron threads
25g/1oz butter
2 shallots, finely chopped
30ml/2 tbsp white wine
250ml/8fl oz/1 cup double cream
grated rind and juice of ½ lemon
115g/4oz peas
350g/12oz somen noodles
½ bunch chervil, roughly chopped
salt and freshly ground black pepper
grated Parmesan cheese (optional)

1 Cut off the asparagus tips (about 5cm/2in in length), then slice the remaining spears into short rounds. Steep the saffron in 30ml/2 tbsp boiling water in a cup.

2 Melt the butter in a saucepan, add the shallots and cook over a low heat for 3 minutes until soft. Add the white wine, cream and saffron infusion. Bring to the boil, reduce the heat and simmer gently for 5 minutes or until the sauce thickens to a coating consistency. Add the grated lemon rind and juice, with salt and pepper to taste.

3 Bring a large saucepan of lightly salted water to the boil. Blanch the asparagus tips, scoop them out and add them to the sauce, then cook the peas and short asparagus rounds in the boiling water until just tender. Scoop them out and add to the sauce.

4 Cook the somen noodles in the same water until just tender, following the directions on the packet. Drain, place in a wide pan and pour the sauce over the top.

5 Toss the noodles with the sauce and vegetables, adding the chervil and more salt and pepper if needed. Finally, sprinkle with the grated Parmesan, if using, and serve hot.

Buckwheat Noodles with Smoked Trout

The light, crisp texture of the bok choy balances the earthy flavours of the mushrooms, the buckwheat noodles and the smokiness of the trout.

INGREDIENTS

Serves 4

350g/12oz buckwheat noodles
30ml/2 tbsp vegetable oil
115g/4oz fresh shiitake
   mushrooms, quartered
2 garlic cloves, finely chopped
15ml/1 tbsp grated fresh
   root ginger
225g/8oz bok choy
1 spring onion, finely
   sliced diagonally
15ml/1 tbsp dark sesame oil
30ml/2 tbsp mirin
30ml/2 tbsp soy sauce
2 smoked trout, skinned and boned
salt and freshly ground black pepper
30ml/2 tbsp coriander leaves and
   10ml/2 tsp sesame seeds, toasted,
   to garnish

1 Cook the buckwheat noodles in a saucepan of boiling water for about 7–10 minutes or until just tender, following the directions on the packet.

2 Meanwhile heat the oil in a large frying pan. Add the shiitake mushrooms and sauté over a medium heat for 3 minutes. Add the garlic, ginger and bok choy, and continue to sauté for 2 minutes.

3 Drain the noodles and add them to the mushroom mixture with the spring onion, sesame oil, mirin and soy sauce. Toss and season with salt and pepper to taste.

4 Break the smoked trout in bite-size pieces. Arrange the noodle mixture on individual serving plates. Place the smoked trout on top of the noodles.

5 Garnish the noodles with coriander leaves and sesame seeds and serve them immediately.

Egg Noodles with Tuna and Tomato Sauce

Raid the store cupboard, add a few fresh ingredients and you can produce a scrumptious main meal in moments.

INGREDIENTS

Serves 4

45ml/3 tbsp olive oil
2 garlic cloves, finely chopped
2 dried red chillies, seeded and chopped
1 large red onion, finely sliced
175g/6oz canned tuna, drained
115g/4oz pitted black olives
400g/14oz can plum tomatoes, mashed, or 400g/14oz can chopped tomatoes
30ml/2 tbsp chopped parsley
350g/12oz medium-thick noodles
salt and freshly ground black pepper

1 Heat the oil in a large frying pan. Add the garlic and dried chillies; fry for a few seconds before adding the sliced onion. Fry, stirring, for about 5 minutes until the onion softens.

2 Add the tuna and black olives to the pan and stir until well mixed. Stir in the tomatoes and any juices. Bring to the boil, season with salt and pepper, add the parsley, then lower the heat and simmer gently.

3 Meanwhile, cook the noodles in boiling water until just tender, following the directions on the packet. Drain well, toss the noodles with the sauce and serve at once.

Stir-fried Noodles with Wild Mushrooms

The greater the variety of wild mushrooms you have available, the more interesting this dish will be. Of course, if you can't find wild mushrooms, then a mixture of cultivated mushrooms can be used instead.

INGREDIENTS

Serves 4

350g/12oz broad flat egg noodles
45ml/3 tbsp vegetable oil
115g/4oz rindless back or streaky bacon, cut into small pieces
225g/8oz wild mushrooms, trimmed and cut in half
115g/4oz garlic chives, snipped
225g/8oz beansprouts
15ml/1 tbsp oyster sauce
15ml/1 tbsp soy sauce
salt and freshly ground black pepper

1 Cook the noodles in a large saucepan of boiling water for about 3–4 minutes or until just tender. Drain, rinse under cold water and drain well.

2 Heat 15ml/1tbsp of the oil in a wok or large frying pan. Add the bacon and fry until golden.

3 Using a slotted spoon, transfer the cooked bacon to a small bowl and set aside until needed.

4 Add the rest of the oil to the wok or pan. When hot, add the mushrooms and fry for 3 minutes. Add the garlic chives and beansprouts to the wok and fry for 3 minutes, then add the drained noodles.

5 Season with salt, pepper, oyster sauce and soy sauce. Continue to stir-fry until the noodles are thoroughly heated through. Sprinkle the crispy bits of bacon on top and serve.

VEGETARIAN NOODLE DISHES

Noodles seem the obvious choice for quick, easy vegetarian dishes, but how many cooks make the most of the many varieties available? The nutty, rather earthy flavour of buckwheat noodles, for instance, provides the perfect foil for creamy goat's cheese, while somen noodles, rice vermicelli and cellophane noodles are equally worthy of investigation. Noodles are low in calories and a good source of complex carbohydrates and fibre. Combined with crisp vegetables and protein in the form of bean curd (tofu), they make a healthy, well-balanced meal.

Cheat's Shark's Fin Soup

Shark's fin soup is a renowned delicacy. In this poor man's vegetarian version cellophane noodles, cut into short lengths, mimic shark's fin needles.

INGREDIENTS

Serves 4–6
4 dried Chinese mushrooms
25ml/1½ tbsp dried wood ears
115g/4oz cellophane noodles
30ml/2 tbsp vegetable oil
2 carrots, cut into fine strips
115g/4oz canned bamboo shoots,
  rinsed, drained and cut into fine strips
1 litre/1¾ pints/4 cups vegetable stock
15ml/1 tbsp soy sauce
15ml/1 tbsp arrowroot or potato flour
30ml/2 tbsp water
1 egg white, beaten (optional)
5ml/1 tsp sesame oil
salt and freshly ground black pepper
2 spring onions, finely chopped,
  to garnish
Chinese red vinegar, to serve (optional)

1 Soak the mushrooms and wood ears separately in warm water for 20 minutes. Drain well. Remove and discard stems from the mushrooms and slice the caps thinly. Cut the wood ears into fine strips, discarding any hard bits. Soak the noodles in hot water until soft. Drain and cut into short lengths. Leave until required.

2 Heat the oil in a large saucepan. Add the mushrooms and stir-fry for 2 minutes. Add the wood ears, stir-fry for 2 minutes, then stir in the carrots, bamboo shoots and noodles.

3 Add the stock to the pan. Bring to the boil, reduce the heat and simmer gently for 15–20 minutes. Season with salt, pepper and soy sauce.

4 Blend the arrowroot or potato flour with a little water. Pour into the soup, stirring all the time to prevent lumps from forming as the soup continues to simmer.

5 Remove the pan from the heat. Stir in the egg white if using, so that it sets to form small threads in the hot soup. Stir in the sesame oil, then pour the soup into individual bowls. Sprinkle each portion with chopped spring onions and offer the Chinese red vinegar separately, if using.

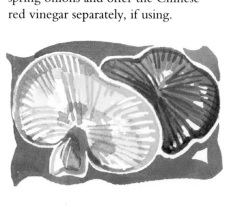

Fried Wontons

These delicious vegetarian versions of the classic wontons are filled with bean curd, spring onions, garlic and ginger.

INGREDIENTS

Makes 30
30 wonton wrappers
1 egg, beaten
oil for deep frying

For the filling
10ml/2 tsp vegetable oil
15ml/1 tbsp grated fresh root ginger
2 garlic cloves, finely chopped
225g/8oz firm bean curd
6 spring onions, finely chopped
10ml/2 tsp sesame oil
15ml/1 tbsp soy sauce
salt and freshly ground black pepper

For the dipping sauce
30ml/2 tbsp soy sauce
15ml/1 tbsp sesame oil
15ml/1 tbsp rice vinegar
2.5ml/½ tsp chilli oil
2.5ml/½ tsp honey
30ml/2 tbsp water

1 Line a large baking sheet with greaseproof paper or sprinkle lightly with flour, then set aside. To make the filling, heat the oil in a frying pan. Add the root ginger and garlic cloves and fry for 30 seconds. Crumble in the bean curd and stir-fry for a few minutes.

2 Add the spring onions, sesame oil and soy sauce to the pan. Stir well and taste for seasoning. Remove from the heat and set aside to cool.

3 Make the dipping sauce by combining all the ingredients in a bowl and mixing well.

4 Place a wonton wrapper on a board in a diamond position. Brush the edges lightly with beaten egg. Spoon 5ml/1 tsp of the filling on the centre of the wonton wrapper.

5 Pull the top corner down to the bottom corner, folding the wrapper over the filling to make a triangle. Press firmly to seal. Place on the prepared baking sheet. Repeat with the rest of the wonton wrappers.

6 Heat the oil in a deep fryer or large saucepan. Carefully add the wontons, a few at a time, and cook for a few minutes until golden brown. Drain on kitchen paper, then serve at once with the dipping sauce.

Vegetable and Egg Noodle Ribbons

Serve this elegant, colourful dish with a tossed green salad as a light lunch or as a starter for six to eight people.

INGREDIENTS

Serves 4
1 large carrot, peeled
2 courgettes
50g/2oz butter
15ml/1 tbsp olive oil
6 fresh shiitake mushrooms, finely sliced
50g/2oz frozen peas, thawed
350g/12oz broad egg ribbon noodles
10ml/2 tsp chopped mixed herbs (such as marjoram, chives and basil)
salt and freshly ground black pepper
25g/1oz Parmesan cheese, to serve (optional)

1 Using a vegetable peeler, carefully slice thin strips from the carrot and from the courgettes.

2 Heat the butter with the olive oil in a large frying pan. Stir in the carrots and shiitake mushrooms; fry for 2 minutes. Add the courgettes and peas and stir-fry until the courgettes are cooked, but still crisp. Season with salt and pepper.

3 Meanwhile, cook the noodles in a large saucepan of boiling water until just tender. Drain the noodles well and tip them into a bowl. Add the vegetables and toss to mix.

4 Sprinkle over the fresh herbs and season to taste. If using the Parmesan cheese, grate or shave it over the top. Toss lightly and serve.

Buckwheat Noodles with Goat's Cheese

When you don't feel like doing a lot of cooking, try this good fast supper dish. The earthy flavour of buckwheat goes well with the nutty, peppery taste of rocket leaves, offset by the deliciously creamy goat's cheese.

INGREDIENTS

Serves 4
350g/12oz buckwheat noodles
50g/2oz butter
2 garlic cloves, finely chopped
4 shallots, sliced
75g/3oz hazelnuts, lightly roasted and roughly chopped
large handful rocket leaves
175g/6oz goat's cheese
salt and freshly ground black pepper

1 Cook the noodles in a large saucepan of boiling water until just tender. Drain well.

2 Heat the butter in a large frying pan. Add the garlic and shallots and cook for 2–3 minutes, stirring all the time, until the shallots are soft.

3 Add the hazelnuts and fry for about 1 minute. Add the rocket leaves and, when they start to wilt, toss in the noodles and heat through.

4 Season with salt and pepper. Crumble in the goat's cheese and serve immediately.

Vegetarian Fried Noodles

When making this dish for non-vegetarians, or for vegetarians who eat fish, add a piece of *blacan* (compressed shrimp paste). A small chunk about the size of a stock cube, mashed with the chilli paste, will add a deliciously rich, aromatic flavour.

INGREDIENTS

Serves 4
2 eggs
5ml/1 tsp chilli powder
5ml/1 tsp turmeric
60ml/4 tbsp vegetable oil
1 large onion, finely sliced
2 red chillies, seeded and
  finely sliced
15ml/1 tbsp soy sauce
2 large cooked potatoes, cut into
  small cubes
6 pieces fried bean curd, sliced
225g/8oz beansprouts
115g/4oz green beans, blanched
350g/12oz fresh thick egg noodles
salt and freshly ground black pepper
sliced spring onions, to garnish

1 Beat the eggs lightly, then strain them into a bowl. Heat a lightly greased omelette pan. Pour in half of the egg to cover the bottom of the pan thinly. When the egg is just set, turn the omelette over and fry the other side briefly. Slide on to a plate, blot with kitchen paper, roll up and cut into narrow strips. Make a second omelette in the same way and slice. Set the omelette strips aside for the garnish.

COOK'S TIP

Always be very careful when handling chillies. Keep your hands away from your eyes as chillies will sting them. Wash your hands thoroughly after touching chillies.

2 In a cup, mix together the chilli powder and turmeric. Form a paste by stirring in a little water.

3 Heat the oil in a wok or large frying pan. Fry the onion until soft. Reduce the heat and add the chilli paste, sliced chillies and soy sauce. Fry for 2–3 minutes.

4 Add the potatoes and fry for about 2 minutes, mixing well with the chillies. Add the bean curd, then the beansprouts, green beans and noodles.

5 Gently stir-fry until the noodles are evenly coated and heated through. Take care not to break up the potatoes or the bean curd. Season with salt and pepper. Serve hot, garnished with the reserved omelette strips and spring onion slices.

Chinese Mushrooms with Cellophane Noodles

Red fermented bean curd adds extra flavour to this hearty vegetarian dish. It is brick red in colour, with a very strong, cheesy flavour, and is made by fermenting bean curd (tofu) with salt, red rice and rice wine. Look out for it in cans or earthenware pots at Chinese food markets.

INGREDIENTS

Serves 4

115g/4oz dried Chinese mushrooms
25g/1oz dried wood ears
115g/4oz dried bean curd
30ml/2 tbsp vegetable oil
2 garlic cloves, finely chopped
2 slices fresh root ginger,
  finely chopped
10 Szechuan peppercorns, crushed
15ml/1 tbsp red fermented bean curd
1/2 star anise
pinch of sugar
15–30ml/1–2 tbsp soy sauce
50g/2oz cellophane noodles, soaked in
  hot water until soft
salt

1 Soak the Chinese mushrooms and wood ears separately in bowls of hot water for 30 minutes. Break the dried bean curd into small pieces and soak in water according to the instructions on the packet.

COOK'S TIP

If you can't find Szechuan peppercorns, then use ordinary black ones instead.

2 Strain the mushrooms, reserving the liquid. Squeeze as much liquid from the mushrooms as possible, then discard the mushroom stems. Cut the cups in half if they are large.

3 The wood ears should swell to five times their original size. Drain them, rinse thoroughly and drain again. Cut off any gritty parts, then cut each wood ear into two or three pieces.

4 Heat the oil in a heavy-based pan. Add the garlic, ginger and Szechuan peppercorns. Fry for a few seconds, then add the mushrooms and red fermented bean curd. Mix lightly and fry for 5 minutes.

5 Add the reserved mushroom liquid to the pan, with sufficient water to completely cover the mushrooms. Add the star anise, sugar and soy sauce, then cover and simmer for 30 minutes.

6 Add the chopped wood ears and reconstituted bean curd pieces to the pan. Cover and cook for about 10 minutes.

7 Drain the cellophane noodles, add them to the mixture and cook for a further 10 minutes until tender, adding more liquid if necessary. Add salt to taste and serve.

Tomato Noodles with Fried Egg

INGREDIENTS

Serves 4

350g/12oz medium-thick
  dried noodles
60ml/4 tbsp vegetable oil
2 garlic cloves, very
  finely chopped
4 shallots, chopped
2.5ml/½ tsp chilli powder
5ml/1 tsp paprika
2 carrots, finely diced
115g/4oz button mushrooms,
  quartered
50g/2oz peas
15ml/1 tbsp tomato ketchup
10ml/2 tsp tomato purée
salt and freshly ground black pepper
butter for frying
4 eggs

1 Cook the noodles in a saucepan of boiling water until just tender. Drain, rinse under cold running water and drain well.

2 Heat the oil in a wok or large frying pan. Add the garlic, shallots, chilli powder and paprika. Stir-fry for about 1 minute, then add the carrots, mushrooms and peas. Continue to stir-fry until the vegetables are cooked.

3 Stir the tomato ketchup and purée into the vegetable mixture. Add the noodles and cook over a medium heat until the noodles are heated through and have taken on the reddish tinge of the paprika and tomato.

4 Meanwhile melt the butter in a frying pan and fry the eggs. Season the noodle mixture, divide it among four serving plates and top each portion with a fried egg.

Curry Fried Noodles

On its own bean curd (tofu) has a fairly bland flavour, but it takes on the flavour of the curry spices wonderfully.

INGREDIENTS

Serves 4

60ml/4 tbsp vegetable oil
30–45ml/2–3 tbsp curry paste
225g/8oz smoked bean curd, cut into
  2.5cm/1in cubes
225g/8oz green beans, cut into
  2.5cm/1in lengths
1 red pepper, seeded and cut into
  fine strips
350g/12oz rice vermicelli, soaked in
  warm water until soft
15ml/1 tbsp soy sauce
salt and freshly ground black pepper
2 spring onions, finely sliced, 2 red
  chillies, seeded and chopped, and
  1 lime, cut into wedges, to garnish

1 Heat half the oil in a wok or large frying pan. Add the curry paste and stir-fry for a few minutes, then add the bean curd and continue to fry until golden brown. Using a slotted spoon remove the cubes from the pan and set aside until required.

2 Add the remaining oil to the wok or pan. When hot, add the green beans and red pepper. Stir-fry until the vegetables are cooked. You may need to moisten them with a little water.

3 Drain the noodles and add them to the wok or frying pan. Continue to stir-fry until the noodles are heated through, then return the curried bean curd to the wok. Season with soy sauce, salt and pepper.

4 Transfer the mixture to a serving dish. Sprinkle with the spring onions and chillies and serve the lime wedges on the side.

Somen Noodles with Courgettes

A colourful dish with lots of flavour. Pumpkin or patty pan squashes can be used as an alternative to courgettes.

INGREDIENTS

Serves 4
2 yellow courgettes
2 green courgettes
60ml/4 tbsp pine nuts
60ml/4 tbsp extra virgin olive oil
2 shallots, finely chopped
2 garlic cloves, finely chopped
30ml/2 tbsp capers, rinsed
4 sun-dried tomatoes in oil, drained
    and cut into strips
300g/11oz somen noodles
60ml/4 tbsp chopped mixed herbs
    (such as chives, thyme and tarragon)
grated rind of 1 lemon
50g/2oz Parmesan cheese, finely grated
salt and freshly ground black pepper

1 Slice the courgettes diagonally into rounds the same thickness as the noodles. Cut the courgette slices into matchsticks. Toast the pine nuts in an ungreased frying pan over a medium heat until golden in colour.

2 Heat half the oil in a large frying pan. Add the shallots and garlic and fry until fragrant. Push the shallot mixture to one side of the pan, add the remaining oil and, when hot, stir-fry the courgettes until soft.

3 Stir thoroughly to incorporate the shallot mixture and add the capers, sun-dried tomatoes and pine nuts. Remove the pan from the heat.

4 Cook the noodles in a large saucepan of boiling, salted water until just tender, following the directions on the packet. Drain well and toss into the courgette mixture, adding the herbs, lemon rind and Parmesan, with salt and pepper to taste. Serve at once.

Noodles Primavera

INGREDIENTS

Serves 4
225g/8oz dried rice noodles
115g/4oz broccoli florets
1 carrot, finely sliced
225g/8oz asparagus, cut into
    5cm/2in lengths
1 red or yellow pepper, seeded and cut
    into strips
50g/2oz baby corn cobs
50g/2oz sugar snap peas, topped
    and tailed
45ml/3 tbsp olive oil
15ml/1 tbsp chopped fresh ginger
2 garlic cloves, chopped
2 spring onions, finely chopped
450g/1lb tomatoes, chopped
1 bunch rocket leaves
soy sauce, to taste
salt and freshly ground black pepper

1 Soak the noodles in hot water for about 30 minutes until soft. Drain.

2 Blanch the broccoli florets, sliced carrot, asparagus, pepper strips, baby corn cobs and sugar snap peas separately in boiling, salted water. Drain them, rinse under cold water, then drain again and set aside.

3 Heat the olive oil in a frying pan. Add the ginger, garlic and onions. Stir-fry for 30 seconds, then add the tomatoes and stir-fry for 2–3 minutes.

4 Add the noodles and stir-fry for 3 minutes. Toss in the blanched vegetables and rocket leaves. Season with soy sauce, salt and pepper and cook until the vegetables are tender.

FAST FRIED NOODLES

The wok is ideal for stir-frying because the thin metal heats quickly and it is deep and wide enough to prevent food from spilling when stirred vigorously. Ingredients must be chopped or sliced thinly to uniform size so that they cook evenly when tossed in hot oil over intense heat. Mee Krob, a classic Thai dish which consists of deep-fried rice vermicelli tossed in a piquant sweet and sour sauce is a good choice for entertaining, but fried noodles also have an everyday role, as when used as a coating for meatballs or fish.

Soft Fried Noodles

This is a very basic dish for serving as an accompaniment or for those occasions when you are feeling a little peckish and fancy something simple. Break an egg into the noodles if you want to add protein. They are also good tossed with oyster sauce and a dollop of chilli black bean sauce.

INGREDIENTS

Serves 4–6
350g/12oz dried egg noodles
30ml/2 tbsp vegetable oil
30ml/2 tbsp finely chopped
    spring onions
soy sauce, to taste
salt and freshly ground black pepper

1 Cook the noodles in a large saucepan of boiling water until just tender, following the directions on the packet. Drain, rinse under cold running water and drain again thoroughly.

2 Heat the oil in a wok and swirl it around. Add the spring onions and fry for 30 seconds. Add the noodles, stirring gently to separate the strands.

3 Reduce the heat and fry the noodles until they are heated through, lightly browned and crisp on the outside, but still soft inside.

4 Season with soy sauce, salt and pepper. Serve at once.

Egg Fried Noodles

Yellow bean sauce gives these noodles a savoury flavour.

INGREDIENTS

Serves 4–6
350g/12oz medium-thick egg noodles
60ml/4 tbsp vegetable oil
4 spring onions, cut into
    1 cm/¹⁄₂ in rounds
juice of 1 lime
15ml/1 tbsp soy sauce
2 garlic cloves, finely chopped
175g/6oz skinless, boneless chicken
    breast, sliced
175g/6oz raw prawns, peeled
    and deveined
175g/6oz squid, cleaned and cut into
    rings (see page 21)
15ml/1 tbsp yellow bean sauce
15ml/1 tbsp fish sauce
15ml/1 tbsp soft light brown sugar
2 eggs
coriander leaves, to garnish

1 Cook the noodles in a saucepan of boiling water until just tender, then drain well and set aside.

2 Heat half the oil in a wok or large frying pan. Add the spring onions, stir-fry for 2 minutes, then add the noodles, lime juice and soy sauce and stir-fry for 2–3 minutes. Transfer the mixture to a bowl and keep warm.

3 Heat the remaining oil in the wok or pan. Add the garlic, chicken, prawns and squid. Stir-fry over a high heat until cooked.

4 Stir in the yellow bean paste, fish sauce and sugar, then break the eggs into the mixture, stirring gently until they set.

5 Add the noodles, toss lightly to mix, and heat through. Serve garnished with coriander leaves.

Rice Noodles with Beef and Black Bean Sauce

This is an excellent combination – beef with a chilli sauce tossed with silky smooth rice noodles.

INGREDIENTS

Serves 4

450g/1lb fresh rice noodles
60ml/4 tbsp vegetable oil
1 onion, finely sliced
2 garlic cloves, finely chopped
2 slices fresh root ginger,
    finely chopped
225g/8oz mixed peppers, seeded and
    cut into strips
350g/12oz rump steak, finely sliced
    against the grain
45ml/3 tbsp fermented black beans,
    rinsed in warm water, drained
    and chopped
30ml/2 tbsp soy sauce
30ml/2 tbsp oyster sauce
15ml/1 tbsp chilli black bean sauce
15ml/1 tbsp cornflour
120ml/4fl oz/½ cup stock or water
2 spring onions, finely chopped, and
    2 red chillies, seeded and finely
    sliced, to garnish

1 Rinse the noodles under hot water; drain well. Heat half the oil in a wok or large frying pan, swirling it around. Add the onion, garlic, ginger and mixed pepper strips. Stir-fry for 3–5 minutes, then remove with a slotted spoon and keep hot.

2 Add the remaining oil to the wok. When hot, add the sliced beef and fermented black beans and stir-fry over a high heat for 5 minutes or until they are cooked.

3 In a small bowl, blend the soy sauce, oyster sauce and chilli black bean sauce with the cornflour and stock or water until smooth. Add the mixture to the wok, then return the onion mixture to the wok and cook, stirring, for 1 minute.

4 Add the noodles and mix lightly. Stir over a medium heat until the noodles are heated through. Adjust the seasoning if necessary. Serve at once, garnished with the chopped spring onions and chillies.

Fried Cellophane Noodles

INGREDIENTS

Serves 4

175g/6oz cellophane noodles
45ml/3 tbsp vegetable oil
3 garlic cloves, finely chopped
115g/4oz cooked prawns, peeled
2 lap cheong, rinsed, drained and
   finely diced
2 eggs
2 celery sticks, including leaves, diced
115g/4oz beansprouts
115g/4oz spinach, cut into
   large pieces
2 spring onions, chopped
15–30ml/1–2 tbsp fish sauce
5ml/1 tsp sesame oil
15ml/1 tbsp sesame seeds, toasted,
   to garnish

1 Soak the cellophane noodles in hot water for about 10 minutes or until soft. Drain and cut the noodles into 10cm/4in lengths.

2 Heat the oil in a wok, add the garlic and fry until golden brown. Add the prawns and lap cheong; stir-fry for 2–3 minutes. Stir in the noodles and fry for 2 minutes more.

3 Make a well in the centre of the prawn mixture, break in the eggs and slowly stir them until they are creamy and just set.

COOK'S TIP

This is a very versatile dish. Vary the vegetables if you wish and substitute ham, chorizo or salami for the lap cheong.

4 Stir in the celery, beansprouts, spinach and spring onions. Season with fish sauce and stir in the sesame oil. Continue to stir-fry until all the ingredients are cooked, mixing well.

5 Transfer to a serving dish. Sprinkle with sesame seeds to garnish.

Savoury Rice Vermicelli

INGREDIENTS

Serves 4

60ml/4 tbsp vegetable oil
1 large onion, finely sliced
2–4 dried red chillies, finely ground
30ml/2 tbsp fermented black beans,
    rinsed, drained and coarsely crushed
2 garlic cloves, finely chopped
30ml/2 tbsp soy sauce
225g/8oz cooked prawns, peeled
6 fried bean curds, sliced
225g/8oz beansprouts
115g/4oz garlic chives, snipped
350g/12oz rice vermicelli, soaked in
    warm water until soft, drained
2 hard-boiled eggs, cut
    into wedges, to garnish

1 Heat half the oil in a wok. Fry the onion with the ground chillies until soft. Add the fermented black beans, garlic and soy sauce. Stir-fry for 1–2 minutes. Add the prawns, bean curd slices, beansprouts and garlic chives. Stir-fry for 1–2 minutes more.

2 Add the vermicelli to the mixture and fry, stirring gently until it is evenly heated through. Taste for seasoning; add more soy sauce if required. Serve the Savoury Rice Vermicelli hot, garnished with the hard-boiled egg wedges.

Stir-fried Beef with Cloud Ears

INGREDIENTS

Serves 4

450g/1lb lean beef (rump or sirloin)
6 dried Chinese mushrooms
15ml/1 tbsp cloud ear mushrooms
30ml/2 tbsp vegetable oil
2 garlic cloves, finely sliced
1 bunch spring onions
coriander leaves, to garnish
4 Fried Loopy Noodles, to serve

For the marinade
5ml/1 tsp grated fresh root ginger
15ml/1 tbsp soy sauce
5ml/1 tsp sesame oil
15ml/1 tbsp oyster sauce
5ml/1 tsp cornflour
salt and freshly ground black pepper

For the sauce
pinch of sugar
5ml/1 tsp dark soy sauce
15ml/1 tbsp oyster sauce
5ml/1 tsp sesame oil
120ml/4fl oz/½ cup Chicken Stock
15ml/1 tbsp cornflour

1 Cut the beef against the grain into fine slices. Mix all the ingredients for the marinade in a shallow dish, add the beef and leave in a cool place to marinate for 1–2 hours. Meanwhile, soak the dried Chinese mushrooms and cloud ear mushrooms in separate bowls of hot water for 30 minutes.

2 Mix all the ingredients for the sauce in a jug or bowl. Set aside.

3 Remove the Chinese mushrooms from the water. Drain them, squeezing out any excess moisture.

4 Remove and discard the stems from the Chinese mushrooms; slice the caps. Drain the cloud ears, trim off any hard woody bits, wash and drain.

5 Heat the oil in a wok. Add the garlic and when it starts to colour, add the beef and all the mushrooms. After 2–3 minutes turn the beef, add the spring onions and mix thoroughly. Make a well in the centre, stir in the sauce mixture and keep turning the mixture over the heat until it thickens. Taste for seasoning. Serve the beef on the Fried Loopy Noodles and garnish with coriander leaves.

Fried Monkfish Coated with Rice Noodles

These marinated medallions of fish are coated in rice vermicelli and deep fried – they taste as good as they look.

INGREDIENTS

Serves 4
450g/1lb monkfish
5ml/1 tsp grated fresh root ginger
1 garlic clove, finely chopped
30ml/2 tbsp soy sauce
175g/6oz rice vermicelli
50g/2oz cornflour
2 eggs, beaten
salt and freshly ground black pepper
oil for deep frying
banana leaves, to serve (optional)

For the dipping sauce
30ml/2 tbsp soy sauce
30ml/2 tbsp rice vinegar
15ml/1 tbsp sugar
2 red chillies, thinly sliced
1 spring onion, thinly sliced

1 Trim the monkfish and cut into 2.5cm/1in thick medallions. Place in a dish and add the ginger, garlic and soy sauce. Mix lightly and leave to marinate for 10 minutes.

2 Meanwhile, make the dipping sauce. Combine the soy sauce, vinegar and sugar in a small saucepan. Bring to the boil. Add salt and pepper to taste. Remove from the heat, add the chillies and spring onion and set aside until required.

3 Using kitchen scissors, cut the noodles into 4cm/1½ in lengths. Spread them out in a shallow bowl.

4 Coat the fish medallions in cornflour, dip in beaten egg and cover with noodles, pressing them on to the fish so that they stick.

5 Deep fry the coated fish in hot oil, 2–3 pieces at a time, until the noodle coating is fluffy, crisp and light golden brown. Drain and serve hot on banana leaves, if you like, accompanied by the dipping sauce.

Crispy Rice Vermicelli

There are a number of variations of this delicious Thai speciality, known locally as *Mee Krob*. In this recipe the noodles are fried until crisp, then stir-fried with sliced chicken and prawns in a piquant chilli sauce.

INGREDIENTS

Serves 4

1 egg, beaten lightly
oil for deep frying
165g/5½ oz thin rice vermicelli
115g/4oz boneless chicken breast, thinly sliced
115g/4oz medium raw prawns, peeled and deveined
3 garlic cloves, finely chopped
2 shallots, finely sliced
30ml/2 tbsp tamarind juice (see Cook's Tip)
15ml/1 tbsp vinegar
60ml/4 tbsp soft light brown sugar
30ml/2 tbsp fish sauce
15ml/1 tbsp brown bean sauce
5ml/1 tsp crushed dried chillies
115g/4oz beansprouts
2 red chillies, seeded and sliced, coriander leaves and snipped chives, to garnish

1 Line a baking sheet with kitchen paper. Heat a lightly greased crêpe pan. Pour in the egg so that it covers the bottom of the pan thinly. When the egg is just set, turn the omelette over and fry the other side briefly. Slide on to a plate, blot with kitchen paper, roll up and cut into narrow strips. Set aside for the garnish.

COOK'S TIP

To make tamarind juice, soak 20ml/ 4 tsp tamarind pulp in 60ml/4 tbsp warm water for 10 minutes; press through a strainer into a jug. Lemon juice can be used as an alternative.

2 Heat the oil in a deep fryer to 190°C/375°F. Break the noodles into fairly short lengths. Drop a large handful of noodles into the oil. Turn them once and remove them as soon as they have swollen and changed colour (this takes seconds, so you have to be quick). Scoop out the noodles and drain. Transfer to the baking sheet. Repeat with the remaining noodles.

3 Transfer 60ml/4 tbsp of the oil to a wok. When the oil is hot, add the chicken and prawns.

4 Stir-fry the chicken and prawns for 3–4 minutes. Remove with a slotted spoon and set aside. Add the garlic and shallots to the oil remaining in the wok; stir-fry until golden.

5 Add the tamarind juice, vinegar, sugar, fish sauce, bean sauce and crushed chillies. Stir to dissolve the sugar, mixing well. Cook the sauce gently until it becomes sticky. Adjust the seasoning for a pleasing balance of sweet, salty and sour.

6 Return the chicken mixture to the sauce and add the fried noodles. Using two spoons, toss the noodles very gently to distribute the sauce and separate any clumps while breaking as few of the noodles as possible.

7 Mound the noodles on a serving platter. Pile the beansprouts at one end of the platter and garnish with the omelette strips, sliced chillies and the coriander leaves and chives.

Fried Loopy Noodles

Serve this as a side dish with any of the toppings in this book. Fried Loopy Noodles also make a crunchy snack at any time and will keep for 4–5 days in an airtight container.

INGREDIENTS

Makes 4–6 coils

175g/6oz flat ribbon noodles
oil for deep frying

1 Cook the noodles in a large saucepan of boiling water until just tender, following the directions on the packet. Rinse under cold water, drain and blot dry using kitchen paper.

2 Heat the oil for deep frying to 190°C/375°F. Using a spoon and fork, form the noodles into coils.

3 Carefully lower the noodle coils into the oil. Deep fry for about 3–4 minutes or until crisp and golden brown. Drain thoroughly on kitchen paper. Pile on to a dish if serving immediately or cool and store as suggested above left.

Crisp Pork Meatballs Laced with Noodles

INGREDIENTS

Serves 4

400g/14oz minced pork
2 garlic cloves, finely chopped
30ml/2 tbsp chopped coriander
  or parsley
15ml/1 tbsp oyster sauce
30ml/2 tbsp fresh breadcrumbs
1 egg, beaten
175g/6oz fresh thin egg noodles
salt and freshly ground black pepper
oil for deep frying
coriander leaves, to garnish
spinach leaves and chilli sauce or
  tomato sauce, to serve

1 In a bowl, mix together the pork, garlic, coriander or parsley, oyster sauce, breadcrumbs and egg. Season with salt and pepper.

2 Knead the pork mixture until sticky, then form into balls about the size of a walnut.

3 Blanch the noodles in a saucepan of boiling water for 2–3 minutes. Drain, rinse under cold running water and drain well.

4 With a meatball in one hand and 3–5 strands of noodles in the other, wrap the noodles securely around the meatball in a criss-cross pattern. Coat the other meatballs in the same way.

5 Deep fry the meatballs in batches in hot oil until golden brown and cooked through in the centre. As each batch browns, remove with a slotted spoon and drain well on kitchen paper. Serve hot on a bed of spinach leaves with chilli sauce or tomato sauce, and garnish with fresh coriander leaves.

SPECIAL OCCASION NOODLES

*Served solo, noodles are quite bland,
but add a tasty sauce, some crisp
vegetables and morsels of meat or fish,
and they are quickly transformed into a
dish fit for the most discerning of diners.
Lightly spiced king prawns with a tang
of lemon grass, served in a rich coconut
sauce, makes a superb dinner party
dish, and the crisp noodle cake on
which it is served will remain a talking
point long after the last mouthful has
been enjoyed. Guests will also relish
Chicken Curry with Rice Vermicelli,
Braised Birthday Noodles with Hoisin
Lamb and the Udon Pot.*

Lemon Grass Prawns on Crisp Noodle Cake

INGREDIENTS

Serves 4

300g/11oz thin egg noodles
60ml/4 tbsp vegetable oil
500g/1¼lb medium raw king prawns,
   peeled and deveined
2.5ml/½ tsp ground coriander
15ml/1 tbsp ground turmeric
2 garlic cloves, finely chopped
2 slices fresh root ginger,
   finely chopped
2 lemon grass stalks, finely chopped
2 shallots, finely chopped
15ml/1 tbsp tomato purée
250ml/8fl oz/1 cup coconut cream
4–6 kaffir lime leaves (optional)
15–30ml/1–2 tbsp fresh lime juice
15–30ml/1–2 tbsp fish sauce
1 cucumber, peeled, seeded and cut
   into 5cm/2in batons
1 tomato, seeded and cut into strips
2 red chillies, seeded and
   finely sliced
salt and freshly ground black pepper
2 spring onions, finely sliced, and
   a few coriander sprigs, to garnish

1 Cook the egg noodles in a saucepan of boiling water until just tender. Drain, rinse under cold running water and drain well.

2 Heat 15ml/1 tbsp of the oil in a large frying pan. Add the noodles, distributing them evenly, and fry for 4–5 minutes until crisp and golden. Turn the noodle cake over and fry the other side. Alternatively, make four individual cakes. Keep hot.

3 In a bowl, toss the prawns with the ground coriander, turmeric, garlic, ginger and lemon grass. Add salt and pepper to taste.

4 Heat the remaining oil in a large frying pan. Add the shallots, fry for 1 minute, then add the prawns and fry for 2 minutes more. Using a slotted spoon remove the prawns.

5 Stir the tomato purée and coconut cream into the mixture remaining in the pan. Stir in lime juice to taste and season with the fish sauce. Bring the sauce to a simmer, return the prawns to the sauce, then add the kaffir lime leaves, if using, and the cucumber. Simmer gently until the prawns are cooked and the sauce is reduced to a nice coating consistency.

6 Add the tomato, stir until just warmed through, then add the chillies. Serve on top of the crisp noodle cake(s), garnished with sliced spring onions and coriander sprigs.

Stir-fried Rice Noodles with Chicken and Prawns

Shellfish have a natural affinity with both meat and poultry. This Thai-style recipe combines chicken with prawns and has the characteristic sweet, sour and salty flavour.

INGREDIENTS

Serves 4

225g/8oz dried flat rice noodles
120ml/4fl oz/½ cup water
60ml/4 tbsp fish sauce
15ml/1 tbsp sugar
15ml/1 tbsp fresh lime juice
5ml/1 tsp paprika
pinch of cayenne pepper
45ml/3 tbsp oil
2 garlic cloves, finely chopped
1 skinless, boneless chicken breast, finely sliced
8 raw prawns, peeled, deveined and cut in half
1 egg
50g/2oz roasted peanuts, coarsely crushed
3 spring onions, cut into short lengths
175g/6oz beansprouts
coriander leaves and 1 lime, cut into wedges, to garnish

1 Place the rice noodles in a large bowl, cover with warm water and soak for 30 minutes until soft. Drain.

2 Combine the water, fish sauce, sugar, lime juice, paprika and cayenne in a small bowl. Set aside until required.

3 Heat the oil in a wok. Add the garlic and fry for 30 seconds until it starts to brown. Add the chicken and prawns and stir-fry for 3–4 minutes until cooked.

4 Push the chicken and prawn mixture in the wok out to the sides. Break the egg into the centre, then quickly stir to break up the yolk and cook over a medium heat until the egg is just lightly scrambled.

5 Add the drained noodles and the fish sauce mixture to the wok. Mix together well. Add half the crushed peanuts and cook, stirring frequently, until the noodles are soft and most of the liquid has been absorbed.

6 Add the spring onions and half of the beansprouts. Cook, stirring for 1 minute more. Spoon on to a platter. Sprinkle with the remaining peanuts and beansprouts. Garnish with the coriander and lime wedges and serve.

Tossed Noodles with Seafood

INGREDIENTS

Serves 4–6

350g/12oz thick egg noodles
60ml/4 tbsp vegetable oil
3 slices fresh root ginger, grated
2 garlic cloves, finely chopped
225g/8oz mussels or clams
225g/8oz raw prawns, peeled
225g/8oz squid, cut into rings
115g/4oz oriental fried fish cake, sliced
1 red pepper, seeded and cut into rings
50g/2oz sugar snap peas, topped
  and tailed
30ml/2 tbsp soy sauce
2.5ml/½ tsp sugar
120ml/4fl oz/½ cup stock or water
15ml/1 tbsp cornflour
5–10ml/1–2 tsp sesame oil
salt and freshly ground black pepper
2 spring onions, chopped, and 2 red
  chillies, seeded and chopped,
  to garnish

1 Cook the noodles in a large saucepan of boiling water until just tender. Drain, rinse under cold water and drain well.

2 Heat the oil in a wok or large frying pan. Fry the ginger and garlic for 30 seconds. Add the mussels or clams, prawns and squid and stir-fry for about 4–5 minutes until the seafood changes colour. Add the fish cake slices, red pepper rings and sugar snap peas and stir well.

3 In a bowl, mix the soy sauce, sugar, stock or water and cornflour. Stir into the seafood and bring to the boil. Add the noodles and cook until they are heated through.

4 Add the sesame oil to the wok or pan and season with salt and pepper to taste. Serve at once, garnished with the spring onions and red chillies.

Noodles with Spicy Meat Sauce

INGREDIENTS

Serves 4–6

30ml/2 tbsp vegetable oil
2 dried red chillies, chopped
5ml/1 tsp grated fresh root ginger
2 garlic cloves, finely chopped
15ml/1 tbsp chilli bean paste
450g/1lb minced pork or beef
450g/1lb broad flat egg noodles
15ml/1 tbsp sesame oil
2 spring onions, chopped, to garnish

For the sauce
1.25ml/¼ tsp salt
5ml/1 tsp sugar
15ml/1 tbsp soy sauce
5ml/1 tsp mushroom ketchup
15ml/1 tbsp cornflour
250ml/8fl oz/1 cup chicken stock
5ml/1 tsp shaohsing wine or
  dry sherry

1 Heat the vegetable oil in a large saucepan. Add the dried chillies, ginger and garlic. Fry until the garlic starts to colour, then gradually stir in the chilli bean paste.

2 Add the minced pork or beef, breaking it up with a spatula or wooden spoon. Cook over a high heat until the minced meat changes colour and any liquid has evaporated.

3 Mix all the sauce ingredients in a jug. Make a well in the centre of the pork mixture. Pour in the sauce mixture and stir together. Simmer for 10–15 minutes until tender.

4 Meanwhile, cook the noodles in a large saucepan of boiling water for 5–7 minutes until just tender. Drain well and toss with the sesame oil. Serve, topped with the meat sauce and garnished with the spring onions.

Stuffed Cabbage Parcels

Served with rice, these attractive, tied parcels make a tasty meal.

INGREDIENTS

Serves 4

4 dried Chinese mushrooms, soaked in
    hot water until soft
50g/2oz cellophane noodles, soaked in
    hot water until soft
450g/1lb minced pork
4 spring onions, finely chopped
2 garlic cloves, finely chopped
30ml/2 tbsp fish sauce
12 large outer green cabbage leaves
4 spring onions
30ml/2 tbsp vegetable oil
1 small onion, finely chopped
2 garlic cloves, crushed
400g/14oz can plum tomatoes
pinch of sugar
salt and freshly ground black pepper

1 Drain the mushrooms, remove and discard the stems and coarsely chop the caps. Put them in a bowl.

2 Drain the noodles and cut them into short lengths. Add the noodles to the bowl with the pork, spring onions and garlic. Season with the fish sauce and add pepper to taste.

3 Cut off the tough stem from each cabbage leaf. Blanch the leaves a few at a time in a saucepan of boiling salted water for about 1 minute. Remove the leaves from the pan and refresh under cold water. Drain and dry on kitchen paper. Add the spring onions to the boiling water and blanch in the same fashion. Drain well.

4 Fill one of the cabbage leaves with a generous spoonful of the pork and noodle filling. Roll up the leaf sufficiently to enclose the filling, then tuck in the sides and continue rolling the leaf to make a tight parcel. Make more parcels in the same way.

5 Split each spring onion lengthways into three strands by cutting through the bulb and then tearing upwards. Tie each of the cabbage parcels with a length of spring onion.

6 Heat the oil in a large frying pan with lid or a flameproof casserole. Add the onion and garlic and fry for 2 minutes or until the onions are soft.

7 Tip the plum tomatoes and their juice into a bowl. Mash the tomatoes with a fork, then stir them into the onion mixture. Season with salt, pepper and a pinch of sugar, then bring to simmering point. Add the cabbage parcels. Cover and cook gently for 20–25 minutes or until the filling is cooked. If at any time the sauce looks a little dry, add some water or stock. Taste the sauce for seasoning and serve at once.

Chicken Curry with Rice Vermicelli

Lemon grass gives this South East Asian curry a wonderful lemony flavour and fragrance.

INGREDIENTS

Serves 4

1 chicken, about 1.5kg/3–3½lb
225g/8oz sweet potatoes
60ml/4 tbsp vegetable oil
1 onion, finely sliced
3 garlic cloves, crushed
30–45ml/2–3 tbsp Thai curry powder
5ml/1 tsp sugar
10ml/2 tsp fish sauce
600ml/1 pint/2½ cups coconut milk
1 lemon grass stalk, cut in half
350g/12oz rice vermicelli, soaked in
   hot water until soft
1 lemon, cut into wedges, to serve

For the garnish

115g/4oz beansprouts
2 spring onions, finely sliced diagonally
2 red chillies, seeded and finely sliced
8–10 mint leaves

1 Skin the chicken. Cut the flesh into small pieces and set aside. Peel the sweet potatoes and cut them into large chunks, about the size of the chicken pieces.

2 Heat half the oil in a large heavy saucepan. Add the onion and garlic and fry until the onion softens.

3 Add the chicken pieces and stir-fry until they change colour. Stir in the curry powder. Season with salt and sugar and mix thoroughly, then stir in the fish sauce.

4 Pour in the coconut milk and add the lemon grass. Cook over a low heat for 15 minutes.

5 Meanwhile, heat the remaining oil in a large frying pan. Fry the sweet potatoes until lightly golden. Using a slotted spoon, add them to the chicken. Cook for 10–15 minutes more, or until both the chicken and sweet potatoes are tender.

6 Drain the rice vermicelli and cook it in a saucepan of boiling water for 3–5 minutes. Drain well. Place in shallow bowls, with the chicken curry. Garnish with beansprouts, spring onions, chillies and mint leaves and serve with lemon wedges.

Braised Birthday Noodles with Hoisin Lamb

In China, the egg symbolizes continuity and fertility so it is frequently included in birthday dishes. The noodles traditionally served at birthday celebrations are left long: it is considered bad luck to cut them since this might shorten one's life.

INGREDIENTS

Serves 4

350g/12oz thick egg noodles
1kg/2¼lb lean neck fillets of lamb
30ml/2 tbsp vegetable oil
115g/4oz fine green beans, topped and
    tailed, and blanched
salt and freshly ground black pepper
2 hard-boiled eggs, halved, and
    2 spring onions, finely chopped,
    to garnish

For the marinade

2 garlic cloves, crushed
10ml/2 tsp grated fresh root ginger
30ml/2 tbsp soy sauce
30ml/2 tbsp rice wine
1–2 dried red chillies
30ml/2 tbsp vegetable oil

For the sauce

15ml/1 tbsp cornflour
30ml/2 tbsp soy sauce
30ml/2 tbsp rice wine
grated rind and juice of ½ orange
15ml/1 tbsp hoisin sauce
15ml/1 tbsp wine vinegar
5ml/1 tsp soft light brown sugar

1 Bring a large saucepan of water to the boil. Add the noodles and cook for 2 minutes only. Drain, rinse under cold water and drain again. Set aside.

2 Cut the lamb into 5cm/2in thick medallions. Mix the ingredients for the marinade in a large shallow dish. Add the lamb and leave to marinate for at least 4 hours or overnight.

3 Heat the oil in a heavy-based saucepan or flameproof casserole. Fry the lamb for 5 minutes until browned. Add just enough water to cover the meat. Bring to the boil, skim, then reduce the heat and simmer for 40 minutes or until the meat is tender, adding more water as necessary.

4 Make the sauce. Blend the cornflour with the remaining ingredients in a bowl. Stir into the lamb and mix well without breaking up the meat.

5 Add the noodles to the lamb with the beans. Simmer gently until both the noodles and the beans are cooked. Add salt and pepper to taste. Divide the noodles among four large bowls, garnish each portion with half a hard-boiled egg, sprinkle with spring onions and serve.

SWEET SURPRISES

Noodles for dessert? The idea may not initially inspire, but some delicious puddings are pasta-based. Try, for instance, warm and comforting Classic Noodle Pudding, based on a traditional Jewish recipe, or Seviyan – an Indian dessert. Caramelized Apple and Rhubarb Noodle Pudding mixes macaroni and fruit with a wonderful rich cream cheese sauce. There are also several new inventions using wonton wrappers, like Date and Walnut Crisps and Fried Wontons and Ice Cream.

Date and Walnut Crisps

Try this sweet version of fried wontons; they make a truly scrumptious snack or dessert.

INGREDIENTS

Makes about 15
25–30 dried dates, pitted
50g/2oz walnuts
30ml/2 tbsp light brown sugar
pinch of ground cinnamon
30 wonton wrappers
1 egg, beaten
oil for deep frying
mint sprigs, to decorate
icing sugar for dusting

1 Chop the dates and walnuts roughly. Place them in a bowl and add the sugar and cinnamon. Mix well.

2 Lay a wonton wrapper on a flat surface. Centre a spoonful of the filling on the wrapper, brush the edges with beaten egg and cover with a second wrapper. Lightly press the edges together to seal. Make more filled wontons in the same way.

3 Heat the oil for deep frying to 180°C/350°F. Deep fry the wontons, a few at a time, until golden. Do not crowd the pan. Remove them with a slotted spoon and drain on kitchen paper. Serve warm, decorated with mint and dusted with icing sugar.

Sweet Vermicelli

This rich, traditional Indian dessert, *Seviyan,* taken from Charmain Soloman's *The Complete Asian Cookbook,* is delicately flavoured with saffron. In India it is traditionally served during the *Eid-ul-Fitr* festival.

INGREDIENTS

Serves 4
60ml/4 tbsp ghee (clarified butter)
115g/4oz rice vermicelli, broken into short lengths
1.25ml/¼ tsp saffron strands
350ml/12fl oz/1½ cups hot water or milk
75g/3oz sugar
30ml/2 tbsp sultanas
30ml/2 tbsp slivered blanched almonds
pinch of ground cardamom
120ml/4fl oz/½ cup whipping cream, whipped
15ml/1 tbsp pistachio nuts, skinned and coarsely chopped

1 Heat the ghee in a heavy-based saucepan. Add the vermicelli and fry until golden brown, tossing lightly so that it colours evenly.

2 Stir the saffron strands into the hot water or milk, then pour on to the vermicelli and bring slowly to the boil. Reduce the heat to low, cover the pan and simmer gently until the vermicelli is just cooked.

3 Add the sugar and sultanas to the vermicelli mixture. Continue to cook, uncovered, until all the liquid has been absorbed.

4 Stir in the slivered almonds and cardamom, mixing well. Serve the vermicelli warm. Add a dollop of whipped cream to each portion and sprinkle with pistachio nuts.

Classic Noodle Pudding

A traditional Jewish recipe, Classic Noodle Pudding is a rich and comforting dessert. It is also quite delicious.

Ingredients

Serves 4–6

175g/6oz wide egg noodles
225g/8oz cottage cheese
115g/4oz cream cheese
75g/3oz caster sugar
2 eggs
120ml/4fl oz/½ cup soured cream
5ml/1 tsp vanilla essence
pinch of ground cinnamon
pinch of grated nutmeg
2.5ml/½ tsp grated lemon rind
50g/2oz butter
25g/1oz nibbed almonds
25g/1oz fine dried white breadcrumbs
icing sugar for dusting

1 Preheat the oven to 180°C/350°F/ Gas 4. Grease a shallow baking dish. Cook the noodles in a large saucepan of boiling water until just tender. Drain well.

2 Beat the cottage cheese, cream cheese and sugar together in a bowl. Add the eggs, one at a time, and stir in the soured cream. Stir in the vanilla essence, cinnamon, nutmeg and lemon rind.

3 Fold the noodles into the cheese mixture. Spoon into the prepared baking dish and level the surface.

4 Melt the butter in a frying pan. Add the almonds and fry for about 1 minute. Remove from the heat.

5 Stir in the breadcrumbs, mixing well. Sprinkle the mixture over the pudding. Bake for 30–40 minutes or until the mixture is set. Serve hot, dusted with a little icing sugar.

Caramelized Apple and Rhubarb Noodle Pudding

This is delicious hot or cold. The richness is offset by the tart flavours of apple and rhubarb.

INGREDIENTS

Serves 4–6
50g/2oz small macaroni
50g/2oz butter
30ml/2 tbsp soft light brown sugar
2 cooking apples, peeled, cored and cut into eighths
225g/8oz rhubarb, cut into 2.5cm/1in lengths
pinch of ground cinnamon
115g/4oz cream cheese
75g/3oz caster sugar
2 eggs
250ml/8fl oz/1 cup whipping cream
few drops of vanilla essence
pinch of grated nutmeg
icing sugar for dusting

1 Preheat the oven to 180°C/350°F/ Gas 4. Grease one or two shallow baking dishes with a little of the butter. Cook the macaroni in a saucepan of boiling water until just tender. Drain, rinse under cold water and drain well.

2 Melt the remaining butter in a large frying pan, add the brown sugar and stir until it dissolves. Add the apples and rhubarb, stirring to coat. Sprinkle over the cinnamon and cook for 3–5 minutes.

3 In a bowl, beat the cream cheese, caster sugar and eggs together until smooth. Stir in the cream and vanilla. Mix well. Fold in the macaroni and fruit mixture, then spoon the mixture into the prepared dishes.

4 Sprinkle the nutmeg over the top. Set the dishes in a roasting tin, then pour hot water into the roasting tin to a depth of 2.5cm/1in. Bake for about 35 minutes until set. Dust with icing sugar and serve hot.

Wonton Twists

These little twists are perfect when you want a quick snack.

INGREDIENTS

Makes 24
12 wonton wrappers
1 egg, beaten
15ml/1 tbsp black sesame seeds
oil for deep frying
icing sugar for dusting (optional)

1 Cut the wonton wrappers in half and make a lengthways slit in the centre of each piece with a sharp knife.

───── COOK'S TIP ─────

Use ordinary sesame seeds in place of the black ones if you prefer.

2 Take one wonton at a time and pull one end through the slit, stretching it a little as you go.

3 Brush each twist with a little beaten egg. Dip the wonton twists briefly in black sesame seeds to coat them lightly.

4 Heat the oil in a deep fryer or large saucepan to 190°C/375°F. Add a few wonton twists at a time so they do not overcrowd the pan. Fry for about 1–2 minutes on each side until crisp and light golden brown. Remove each twist and drain on kitchen paper. Dust the wonton twists with icing sugar, if you like, and serve at once.

Fried Wontons and Ice Cream

Americans have their cookies and ice cream – here is the Chinese equivalent. Serve it with fresh or poached fruits or fruit sauces for an impressive treat.

INGREDIENTS

Serves 4
oil for deep frying
12 wonton wrappers
8 scoops of your favourite
   ice cream

───── COOK'S TIP ─────

Try using two flavours of ice cream – chocolate and strawberry perhaps, or vanilla and coffee. For a sophisticated adults-only treat, drizzle over a spoonful of your favourite liqueur.

1 Heat the oil in a deep fryer or large saucepan to 190°C/375°F.

2 Add a few wonton wrappers at a time so that they do not crowd the pan too much. Fry for 1–2 minutes on each side until the wrappers are crisp and light golden brown.

3 Leave the cooked wontons to drain on kitchen paper.

4 To serve, place one wonton on each plate. Place a scoop of ice cream on top of each wonton. Top with a second wonton, then add another ball of ice cream and finish with a final wonton. Serve at once.

Index

Apples: caramelized apple and
  rhubarb noodle pudding, 93
Asparagus: noodles with asparagus
  and saffron sauce, 48

Bacon: Shanghai noodles with
  lap cheong, 46
Bean curd: curry fried noodles, 60
Beef: Hanoi beef and noodle soup, 37
  noodles with spicy meat sauce, 80
  rice noodles with beef and black
    bean sauce, 68
  soupy noodles – Malay-style, 40
  stir-fried beef with cloud ears, 70
Black beans: rice noodles with beef
  and black bean sauce, 68
  savoury rice vermicelli, 70
Buckwheat noodles: buckwheat
  noodles with goat's cheese, 56
  buckwheat noodles with smoked
    salmon, 30
  buckwheat noodles with smoked
    trout, 49
  chicken and buckwheat noodle
    soup, 36

Cabbage: stuffed cabbage parcels, 82
Cellophane noodles: cheat's shark's fin
  soup, 54
  Chinese mushrooms with cellophane
    noodles, 59
  clay pot of chilli squid and
    noodles, 21
  fried cellophane noodles, 69
  potato and cellophane noodle
    salad, 29
  prawn noodle salad with fragrant
    herbs, 24
  stuffed cabbage parcels, 82
  Vietnamese spring rolls with nuoc
    cham sauce, 17
Cheese: buckwheat noodles with goat's
  cheese, 56
  cheese fritters, 18
  classic noodle pudding, 92
Chicken: chicken and buckwheat
  noodle soup, 36
  chicken chow mein, 45
  chicken curry with rice vermicelli, 86
  chicken stock, 36
  crispy rice vermicelli, 73
  egg fried noodles, 66
  egg noodle salad with sesame
    chicken, 32
  stir-fried rice noodles with chicken
    and prawns, 79
  udon pot, 84
Chinese greens: Shanghai noodles with
  lap cheong, 46
Chow mein, chicken, 45
  combination chow mein, 84
Clams: tossed noodles with seafood, 80
Classic noodle pudding, 92
Courgettes: somen noodles with
  courgettes, 62
Crab: seafood wontons with coriander
  dressing, 20
  Vietnamese spring rolls with nuoc
    cham sauce, 17
Curry: chicken curry with rice
  vermicelli, 86
  curry fried noodles, 60
  curry fried pork and rice vermicelli
    salad, 28

Date and walnut crisps, 90

Egg noodles: braised birthday noodles
  with hoisin lamb, 87
  classic noodle pudding, 92
  combination chow mein, 84
  crisp pork meatballs laced with
    noodles, 74
  egg fried noodles, 66
  egg noodle salad with sesame
    chicken, 32
  egg noodles with tuna and tomato
    sauce, 50
  lemon grass prawns on crisp noodle
    cake, 78
  noodle soup with pork and Szechuan
    pickle, 38
  noodles with spicy meat sauce, 80
  noodles with tomatoes, sardines and
    mustard, 46
  soft fried noodles, 66
  soupy noodles – Malay-style, 40
  stir-fried noodles with wild
    mushrooms, 50
  tossed noodles with seafood, 80
  vegetable and egg noodle ribbons, 56
  vegetarian fried noodles, 58
Eggs: tomato noodles with fried
  egg, 60

Fried loopy noodles, 74

Ice cream: fried wontons and ice
  cream, 94

Lamb: braised birthday noodles with
  hoisin lamb, 87
Lap cheong: Shanghai noodles with lap
  cheong, 46
Lettuce: lettuce with peanut dressing and
  wonton crisps, 14
  lettuce wraps with sesame noodles, 12

Macaroni: caramelized apple and rhubarb
  noodle pudding, 93
Monkfish: fried monkfish coated with
  rice noodles, 72
Mushrooms: cheat's shark's fin soup, 54
  Chinese mushrooms with cellophane
    noodles, 59
  stir-fried beef with cloud ears, 70
  stir-fried noodles with wild
    mushrooms, 50
Mussels: combination chow mein, 84
  tossed noodles with seafood, 80

Nori seaweed: chilled soba noodles with
  nori, 18

Onions: egg noodles with tuna and
  tomato sauce, 50
  sesame noodles with spring
    onions, 26

Peanuts: lettuce with peanut dressing and
  wonton crisps, 14
  peanut sauce, 13
Pineapple: noodles with pineapple,
  ginger and chillies, 30
Pork: combination chow mein, 84
  crisp pork meatballs laced with
    noodles, 74
  curry fried pork and rice vermicelli
    salad, 28

noodle soup with pork and Szechuan
  pickle, 38
noodles with spicy meat sauce, 80
pork satay with crisp noodle cake, 83
rice noodle and salad rolls, 13
soupy noodles – Malay-style, 40
stuffed cabbage parcels, 82
Vietnamese spring rolls with nuoc
  cham sauce, 17
Potato and cellophane noodle salad, 29
Prawns: combination chow mein, 84
  crispy rice vermicelli, 73
  egg fried noodles, 66
  fried cellophane noodles, 69
  lemon grass prawns on crisp
    noodle cake, 78
  noodles with sun-dried tomatoes
    and prawns, 44
  prawn noodle salad with fragrant
    herbs, 24
  rice vermicelli and salad rolls, 13
  seafood laksa, 41
  seafood wontons with coriander
    dressing, 20
  stir-fried rice noodles with chicken
    and prawns, 79
  tossed noodles with seafood, 80
  udon pot, 84
  Vietnamese spring rolls with nuoc
    cham sauce, 17

Red snapper: snapper, tomato and
  tamarind noodle soup, 38
Rhubarb: caramelized apple and rhubarb
  noodle pudding, 93
Rice noodles: fried monkfish coated
  with rice noodles, 72
  Hanoi beef and noodle soup, 37
  noodles primavera, 62
  rice noodles with beef and black bean
    sauce, 68
  stir-fried rice noodles with chicken
    and prawns, 79
Rice vermicelli: chicken curry with rice
  vermicelli, 86
  crispy rice vermicelli, 73
  curry fried noodles, 60
  curry fried pork and rice vermicelli
    salad, 28
  lettuce wraps with sesame
    noodles, 12
  rice vermicelli and salad rolls, 13
  savoury rice vermicelli, 70
  seafood laksa, 41
  snapper, tomato and tamarind noodle
    soup, 38
Sweet vermicelli, 90

Salad: buckwheat noodles with smoked
  salmon, 30
  curry fried pork and rice
    vermicelli salad, 28 .
  egg noodle salad with sesame
    chicken, 32
  noodles with pineapple, ginger and
    chillies, 30
  potato and cellophane noodle
    salad, 29
  prawn noodle salad with fragrant
    herbs, 24
  rice vermicelli and salad rolls, 13
  sesame noodles with spring onion, 26
  smoked trout and noodle salad, 25
  spicy Szechuan noodles, 26

Thai noodle salad, 33
Sardines: noodles with tomatoes, sardines
  and mustard, 46
Scallops: seared scallops with wonton
  crisps, 16
Shanghai noodles with lap cheong, 46
Smoked salmon: buckwheat noodles
  with smoked salmon, 30
Smoked trout: buckwheat noodles with
  smoked trout, 49
  smoked trout and noodle salad, 25
Soba noodles: chilled soba noodles with
  nori, 18
  sesame noodles with spring
    onions, 26
Somen noodles: noodles with asparagus
  and saffron sauce, 48
  noodles with sun-dried tomatoes and
    prawns, 44
  smoked trout and noodle salad, 25
  somen noodles with baked cherry
    tomatoes, 14
  somen noodles with courgettes, 62
  Thai noodle salad, 33
Soup: cheat's shark's fin soup, 54
  chicken and buckwheat noodle
    soup, 36
  Hanoi beef and noodle soup, 37
  noodle soup with pork and Szechuan
    pickle, 38
  seafood laksa, 41
  snapper, tomato and tamarind noodle
    soup, 38
  soupy noodles – Malay-style, 40
Spicy Szechuan noodles, 26
Squid: clay pot of chilli squid and
  noodles, 21
  combination chow mein, 84
  egg fried noodles, 66
  seafood laksa, 41
  tossed noodles with seafood, 80
Tomatoes: egg noodles with tuna and
  tomato sauce, 50
  noodles with sun-dried tomatoes and
    prawns, 44
  noodles with tomatoes, sardines and
    mustard, 46
  snapper, tomato and tamarind noodle
    soup, 38
  somen noodles with baked cherry
    tomatoes, 14
  tomato noodles with fried egg, 60
Tuna: egg noodles with tuna and tomato
  sauce, 50

Udon noodles: noodles with pineapple,
  ginger and chillies, 30
  udon pot, 84

Vegetables: noodles primavera, 62
  vegetable and egg noodle
    ribbons, 56

Walnuts: date and walnut crisps, 90
Wontons: cheese fritters, 18
  fried wontons and ice cream, 94
  fried wontons, 55
  lettuce with peanut dressing and
    wonton crisps, 14
  seafood wontons with coriander
    dressing, 20
  seared scallops with wonton
    crisps, 16
  wonton twists, 94